Cambridge Elements

Elements in Reinventing Capitalism
edited by
Arie Y. Lewin
Duke University
Till Talaulicar
University of Erfurt

THE POST-MANAGERIAL ERA OF CAPITALISM

Organizational Design as the Next Innovation Frontier

Hunter Hastings
Bialla Venture Partners

Shaftesbury Road, Cambridge CB2 8EA, United Kingdom

One Liberty Plaza, 20th Floor, New York, NY 10006, USA

477 Williamstown Road, Port Melbourne, VIC 3207, Australia

314–321, 3rd Floor, Plot 3, Splendor Forum, Jasola District Centre, New Delhi – 110025, India

103 Penang Road, #05–06/07, Visioncrest Commercial, Singapore 238467

Cambridge University Press is part of Cambridge University Press & Assessment, a department of the University of Cambridge.

We share the University's mission to contribute to society through the pursuit of education, learning and research at the highest international levels of excellence.

www.cambridge.org
Information on this title: www.cambridge.org/9781009608121

DOI: 10.1017/9781009608084

© Hunter Hastings 2025

This publication is in copyright. Subject to statutory exception and to the provisions of relevant collective licensing agreements, no reproduction of any part may take place without the written permission of Cambridge University Press & Assessment.

When citing this work, please include a reference to the DOI 10.1017/9781009608084

First published 2025

A catalogue record for this publication is available from the British Library

ISBN 978-1-009-60812-1 Hardback
ISBN 978-1-009-60811-4 Paperback
ISSN 2634-8950 (online)
ISSN 2634-8942 (print)

Cambridge University Press & Assessment has no responsibility for the persistence or accuracy of URLs for external or third-party internet websites referred to in this publication and does not guarantee that any content on such websites is, or will remain, accurate or appropriate.

For EU product safety concerns, contact us at Calle de José Abascal, 56, 1°, 28003 Madrid, Spain, or email eugpsr@cambridge.org

The Post-Managerial Era of Capitalism

Organizational Design as the Next Innovation Frontier

Elements in Reinventing Capitalism

DOI: 10.1017/9781009608084
First published online: December 2025

Hunter Hastings
Bialla Venture Partners
Author for correspondence: Hunter Hastings, hunterhastings@icloud.com

Abstract: Traditional business management was the machinery of control for industrial organizations that had sprawled beyond the oversight of their founders, an organizational innovation that became a profession and a science. The aim was the stability and predictability the financial sector demanded. But control brought increasing costs: (1) slow response to market changes; leaving established firms behind innovative newcomers; (2) bureaucratic inertia that strangled flexibility; (3) disengaged employees who felt their creativity and agility stifled. These failures weakened firms and lowered economic productivity. In the Kuhnian framework of scientific revolutions, the management paradigm entered crisis mode. Consistent with the Kuhnian framing, businesses are moving beyond management. Self-organization and enterprise flow are revolutionizing business models. Interconnected ecosystems replace bounded industries. Experimentation and feedback replace traditional strategic planning. Dynamic, autonomous teams replace hierarchies of authority. Liberated companies embrace dynamic cohesion rather than the rigidities of business administration. They operate in a post-managerial era.

This Element also has a video abstract: Cambridge.org/RECA_Hunter_abstract

Keywords: post-managerial era, new management paradigm, self-organization, venture mode, entrepreneurship

© Hunter Hastings 2025

ISBNs: 9781009608121 (HB), 9781009608114 (PB), 9781009608084 (OC)
ISSNs: 2634-8950 (online), 2634-8942 (print)

Contents

1 Introduction: A Short History of Management   3

2 The Consequences of Managerial Systems   12

3 Shifting the Paradigm: Anomalies and Crisis   17

4 A New Worldview: Self-organizing Systems   25

5 Pioneers and Experiments   31

6 The Emergent Novelty: Self-management   45

7 The New Technologically Evolved Business Models of Hyper-personalization   50

8 The New Integration of Self-management and Digital Enablement   56

9 Enabling Cohesion: More Freedom, Less Authority   61

10 Conclusion   84

References   88

Foreword

Imagine a world where the heavy machinery of control – born in the smoky factories of the nineteenth century – gives way to a vibrant, living network of human potential. A world where people, not processes, drive progress, and where the rigid hierarchies of traditional management dissolve into fluid, self-organizing systems that pulse with creativity and purpose. This Element is your invitation to step into that world, to witness the dawn of a post-managerial era where freedom, commitment, and adaptability redefine what it means to build thriving organizations. It's a story of liberation, grounded in the science of complexity, fueled by the courage of pioneers, and amplified by the limitless possibilities of digital innovation.

The old paradigm of management, forged by visionaries like George Whistler and Frederick W. Taylor, was a triumph of its time. It brought order to the chaos of sprawling industrial empires, offering predictability that won the trust of financiers and fueled economic growth. But every system carries the seeds of its own obsolescence. The very structures that promised stability – hierarchies, standardized processes, top-down authority – became shackles. They slowed organizations to a crawl in the face of disruptive competitors, choked resource flexibility with bureaucratic inertia, and silenced the creative spark of individuals buried under layers of oversight. These aren't just flaws; they're systemic failures that drain vitality from firms and sap economic potential.

As Thomas Kuhn taught us, when anomalies pile up and the old paradigm can't explain them, a crisis emerges. That crisis is here, and it's shaking the foundations of traditional management to its core. This Element doesn't just diagnose the problem; it lights a path forward. It traces the evolution of management through its phases – control, leadership, technocracy – showing how firms like GE and IBM embodied its principles and reaped its rewards, but also its costs. Then, with the clarity of a Kuhnian lens, it reveals the shift to a new science of organization, one rooted in the principles of complex adaptive systems.

Forget the clockwork precision of Newtonian mechanics; the future belongs to systems that evolve through bottom-up interactions, emergent constraints, and what physicist Adrian Bejan calls flow – the removal of barriers to freedom, one degree at a time. This is a science of life, of adaptation, of possibility. At the heart of this revolution are the pioneers – organizations like W.L. Gore, Semco, Haier, Valve, Buurtzorg, and Morning Star. These aren't just companies; they're experiments in human freedom. Morning Star, where I enjoyed the privilege of contributing, is one part of this story. We operated without bosses, titles, or job descriptions, guided by two simple principles: no one coerces another, and every individual honors their commitments. Our Colleague Letter of Understanding (CLOU) system – where each person defines their voluntary promises to colleagues – didn't come from a boardroom or a consultant's playbook.

Morning Star's form of self-management is a living example of spontaneous order emerging from myriad interactions like water molecules forming clouds, dissipating and re-forming. This isn't theory; it's reality. A company with a billion dollars in sales that enjoys global industry leadership, Morning Star proved that self-management scales, adapts, and thrives. Picture a dynamic, three-dimensional web of commitments, constantly reshaping itself to meet the needs of customers and colleagues, all without a single command from above. That's the power of self-organization.

But the story doesn't stop there. Technology is pushing the boundaries even further, weaving self-management into the fabric of hyper-personalized business models. Digitization has handed power to customers, who now demand exactly what they want, when they want it. Companies like Handu, an Asian e-commerce innovator, show us the future: a front-end of autonomous, entrepreneurial sites, backed by a digitally automated core and a robust infrastructure. Success drives resources, failure fades away, all guided by what a *Harvard Business Review* case calls "digitally enhanced directed autonomy."

This is self-organization on steroids, blending human ingenuity with AI and data to create firms that don't just react – they anticipate. What makes this Element sing is its rejection of the old paradigm's obsession with formulas and checklists. Instead, it offers a pattern – eight emergent characteristics of the post-managerial age, from dynamic cohesion to the liberation of individual potential. This isn't a recipe; it's a worldview. As Kuhn warned, those wedded to the old ways may struggle to see it, but for those ready to embrace a new language of freedom and flow, the horizon is wide open.

This is about weaving constraints into a tapestry that amplifies outcomes, replacing control with enablement. It's about trusting people to do what's right because they're committed to it, not because they're ordered to. This Element isn't just a reflection; it's a call to arms. It challenges you – leader, thinker, doer – to dismantle the barriers that hold back human potential. Learn from the misfits who dared to experiment. Draw from the science of complexity that shows us how systems evolve. Harness technology not to control, but to empower. The result is a vision of work that's deeply human, where purpose and creativity aren't just allowed but unleashed, where organizations move like living organisms, resilient and ever evolving.

We're at a turning point. The future of business isn't about taming complexity; it's about dancing with it. It's not about imposing order; it's about letting order emerge from the commitments and creativity of free individuals. This Element is your guide to that dance, your provocation to join the revolution. The post-managerial age is here, and it's time to step into it with courage and conviction. Welcome to a world where freedom works.

Doug Kirkpatrick
Founder, D'Artagnan Advisors

1 Introduction: A Short History of Management

The twentieth century witnessed a long period of sustained effort to apply method to management. It was a scientific era where positivism – the belief that all legitimate knowledge must be derived from empirical observation and rational analysis – was the dominant intellectual framework. Management sought to align itself with the rigor of the natural sciences, influenced by the towering successes of mathematics and physics. Hard and fast laws were to be established for social sciences like economics and management by following the pathways of measurement, mathematical analysis, and experimental validation.

In fact, the precedents for twentieth-century management were laid down in the nineteenth century. Positivism became Europe's dominant philosophy of science, the belief that all mysteries of the universe can be fully unraveled through scientific inquiry. These European positivist proclivities spilled over into the United States, and caught on strongly. The country that so admired innovation and entrepreneurs generated an immense optimism that science would soon solve all business problems and brilliant technocrats would engineer a new and better world. This positive technocracy was the climate in which management science emerged.

The 1841 Western Railroad Accident and George Whistler's Management System

In October 1841, a serious train accident occurred on the Western Railroad, which connected Albany, New York, and Worcester, Massachusetts. A head-on collision resulted in two deaths and many injuries. Worse than the death and injury toll was the severe jolt the accident gave to the national psyche and people's trust in industrialization. The tragic accident was a wake-up call for the railroad industry, which was in its early stages of development in the United States. The crash revealed not only the inherent dangers of rail travel but also significant gaps in the organization and management of railroads.

The collision was due to poor communication and coordination. Consulting engineer George Whistler identified issues of scheduling, authority, and information flow between personnel, resulting in an environment where mistakes and accidents could easily occur. He judged that the accident underscored the lack of a clear, hierarchical authority structure in railroad management – one that could ensure accountability and the smooth flow of information.

In designing a management solution, Whistler applied his military background and the principles of military organization – specifically, the Prussian military command structure – to the management of the railroad. The Prussian army was known for its emphasis on discipline, clear chains of command, and centralized control, principles that Whistler saw as applicable to the complex and dangerous operations of the railroad.

His design specifically included (1) centralized authority with a clear hierarchy and distinct layers of authority and responsibility; (2) a formal command structure in which train conductors, engineers, and other staff members were given specific roles and responsibilities, with orders flowing from the top down; (3) strict formalized scheduling and timetables; (4) structured reporting of incidents and performance to superiors.

In many ways, we can identify George Whistler and the Prussian military as precursors of the management systems we have inherited. His written report and recommendations were widely circulated through the new class of managers that was just coming into being.

The Foundations of the Management Paradigm

Phase 1: Management for Operational Control

The expression of the principles of Whistler's design for railroad administration took the form of management for operational control of industrial businesses. We can highlight three early prophets who documented this new drive for control.

Frederick Winslow Taylor (1856–1915) was one of the first to employ the positivist view of business – that business managers can engineer maximum efficiency through carefully applied scientific principles – to attempt to establish a discipline of business management, to be studied and applied with methodical precision. In this context, he was "one of the individuals who had the greatest influence on the 20th century" (Alexander, 2020). He aimed at a monopoly for managers of knowledge about work tasks and processes in order to rigidly control them.

His high purpose was "greater national efficiency" (Taylor, 1911), and his method was to dehumanize the work process: "In the past the man has been first; in the future the system must be the first." The remedy for human inefficiency was to be found in the principles of scientific management:

"management is a true science, resting on clearly defined laws, rules and principles as a foundation." He claimed that this science would double the output of each man and each machine, mostly by eliminating the practice of "loafing or soldiering . . . the natural instinct and tendency of men to take it easy."

Taylor's book, *The Principles of Scientific Management*, set out to demolish the old idea that each workman can best regulate his own way of doing the work. The new science of management placed the entire responsibility on management, who were to analyze and standardize work steps and ensure that they were carried out in a predefined sequence at a predefined pace. Workers could be viewed by managers as a kind of machine to be monitored and controlled.

Taylor wrote that "Taylor wrote that "the fundamental principles of scientific management are applicable to all kinds of human activities, from our simplest individual acts to the work of our great corporations. The fundamental principles of scientific management are applicable to all kinds of human activities, from our simplest individual acts to the work of our great corporations."

As he had hoped, Taylor's approach became a standard. It was widely adopted in industry (e.g., by Ford Motor Company in assembly line manufacturing), in World War I military logistics, and in business schools, where courses in scientific management drew heavily on Taylor's work. The Progressive era saw an Efficiency Movement, lauded by leaders such as Andrew Carnegie and John D Rockefeller, and even by President Theodore Roosevelt, whose call for national efficiency was cited as a driver by Taylor in the introduction to *The Principles of Scientific Management*.

Henri Fayol (1841–1925) was a contemporary of Taylor who developed Administrative Management Theory. While Taylor focused on the shop floor and task efficiency, Fayol addressed a different dimension – the overall structure and function of management at the organizational level. He identified five functions of management: planning, organizing, commanding, coordinating, and control (Fayol, 1917). Within the five functions, he found fourteen principles, including Authority and Responsibility, Discipline, Unity of Command, and Subordination (of individual interest to general interest). He also included Esprit de Corps as the last item in the list of fourteen principles! He set out a theory of management based on the fourteen principles and proposed that administrative management could be taught on this basis.

Fayol's management principles led to him being called the father of modern management (Wren, 2002). It has been suggested that Fayol's fourteen principles metamorphosed into present-day management and the burgeoning administrative formation that exhibits itself all across the globe (Uzuegbu, 2015).

Elton Mayo (1880–1949) was a leader in – some say the founder of – the human relations movement within management theory, specifically applying his attention to the behavior of people in groups. Some of his source material came from The Hawthorne Studies, a series of observations and interviews in the 1920s and 1930s in the context of factory assembly of electrical components. The Hawthorne Studies were interpreted through the lenses of the productivity benefits of social dynamics and team cohesion. Mayo saw work as a profoundly social activity, and identified workers' social and psychological needs that management must attend to. Mayo's integration of psychology into his interpretation of motivational and productivity variables emphasized communication, collaboration, and the management of feelings and emotions to encourage compatible relationships in social groups within companies. This more human-centered, psychology-informed approach, emphasizing the importance of interpersonal relationships and group dynamics, can be viewed as an extension of Taylor's and Fayol's focus on the measurement and organization of behavior. It expanded the management paradigm into psychology and informal networks, and supported concepts such as employee engagement. Nevertheless, the goal remained the increase in efficiency and the elimination of variance in performance compared to benchmarks.

We can group (see Table 1) the Taylor, Fayol, and Mayo views of management into a grouping that represents the first phase of the development of the original management paradigm; management for operational control, with the goal of extracting productivity from the workforce.

Paradigm Element	Key Thinker	Focus	Authority model	Legacy
Scientific Management	Frederick Taylor	Task-level efficiency and control	Manager commands, worker obeys	Organizational engineering
Administrative Management	Henri Fayol	Organizational structure and administration	Hierarchy with formal authority	Classical management functions
Human Relations Management	Elton Mayo	Worker morale and social needs	Control through supportive supervision	Organizational Behavior

Table 1 Phase 1: Management as control.

Phase 2: Elevation of Management to Leadership

As management began to evolve into a profession, practiced as a form of control within a context of hierarchical authority, it was allocated social prestige. The concept of management as leadership emerged (see Table 2).

Mary Parker Follett (1863–1933) was one of the most important early influences in establishing leadership as a management concept. She did not recommend eliminating hierarchy, but saw leadership as a management skill that could be exercised as a lateral process in a traditionally vertically organized company. Importantly, leadership power emanated from authority of expertise in addition to position in a hierarchy. In this context, management power could be less coercive and more facilitating, integrating and collaborative ("power with" rather than "power over"), without losing sight of the purpose of "getting things done" (Peek, 2024). In other words, she saw leadership as another form of power to control others. We may think of the concept of leadership in business as a very contemporary idea in the twenty-first century, but Warren Bennis asserted that "Just about everything written today about leadership and organizations comes from Mary Parker Follett's writings and lectures" (Bennis, 2003).

Alfred Chandler (1918–2007) viewed management through the lens of organizational strategy and corporate structure. He was a business historian who documented the path to scale – he referred to mass production, mass

Paradigm Element	Key thinker	Focus	Authority model	Legacy
Management as Leadership	Mary Parker Follett	Reframing power as facilitation	Relational shared authority	Leadership programs
Management of scale and scope	Alfred Chandler	Strategic coordination of control	Centralized bureaucracy	Classic divisionalized structures
Management of knowledge workers	Peter Drucker	Knowledge as resource, labor as knowledge work	Culture is a management domain	Management as a liberal art

Table 2 Phase 2: Control + leadership.

distribution and mass marketing – and plainly admired the achievement of not only the great industrialists who built the large corporations of the late nineteenth and early twentieth centuries, but equally of the appointed executives who took over from the founding entrepreneurs and administered and managed their burgeoning creations. His book titles included *Strategy and Structure* and *Scale and Scope*, and, most tellingly, *The Visible Hand: The Managerial Revolution in American Business*. Chandler defined management as the complex administrative system required to bring cohesion to industrial scale corporations, via the control that could be exerted through organizational design, including hierarchy, top-down systems, integration achieved through divisionalization and departmentalization, process documentation, and detailed job descriptions. He proposed a managerial revolution (the positivist visible hand replacing Adam Smith's subjectivist invisible hand) and the consolidation of a managerial class. While Chandler did not write much about "how to manage," he did a lot to further elevate the profession of management to the highest levels of aspiration. It was a practice of the largest, and therefore best, corporations, to be admired and emulated.

Peter Drucker (1909–2005) elevated the profession of management to an even higher level of vocation and philosophy. He was dubbed a "management guru" who shaped management practices. One of his biographers elevated him to the position of "champion of management as a serious discipline" (Beatty, 1998). He introduced the term "knowledge worker" (Drucker, 1959), highlighting the intellectual capabilities required for management, and designated management as a "liberal art" (Drucker, 2006), integrating perspectives from philosophy, culture, and sociology. He emphasized the ethical responsibilities of management, as well as execution. This was not a departure from control. His concept of management by objectives established accountability and performance measurement for specific, measurable goals set by the authority levels in the firm. He saw control over resource allocation as crucial for achieving strategic objectives. Cultural alignment was an aspect of "soft" control – Drucker's management cultures were strong in employing norms and shared beliefs to guide employee behavior.

Phase 3: Management by Technocrats

As data and technology became resources to management, the processes and practices of management adopted and integrated them into the scientific method (see Table 3).

Paradigm Element	Key thinker	Focus	Authority model	Legacy
Quality control	W. Edwards Deming	Statistical process control	Data models, continuous monitoring	Quality control studies
Science of Administration	Herbert Simon	Tools, techniques and methods	Scientific business principles	Business administration curricula
Modeling market structure	Michael Porter	Competitive advantage	Strategic management	Centralized strategy planning
Business engineering	Michael Hammer	Process optimization	Process management	Business process reengineering
Change management	John P. Kotter	Business transformation	Managerial elite	Transformation campaigns

Table 3 Phase 3: Technocratic management.

W. Edwards Deming (1900–1993) added another dimension to the managerial control spectrum, that of statistical control. Encapsulated in a theory of Total Quality Management (TQM), Deming's approach was to emphasize a characteristic he called "quality," defined as consistent production without error on a track of continuous improvement measured by systematic data collection and analysis, which together defined a practice known as quality management. He specifically preferred management by numbers to management by objectives (Deming, 1982). Statistical process control became established as a benchmark source for efficiency and productivity assessments.

Herbert Simon (1916–2001) was one of the most influential management scholars. He studied at the University of Chicago, and recalled that, amongst his professional colleagues, "Logical positivism was the dominant, perhaps exclusive religion in this group" (Simon, 1996). Simon's book, *Administrative Behavior*, published in 1945, became the seminal textbook for teaching business administration, now the focus of the MBA. It proposed a fundamentally scientific approach to business management, whereby management scholars can develop tools and proven techniques for managers to apply to engineer better performance and efficiency. He proposed scientific principles of design so that even innovation could be engineered rather than left to the creative whims of entrepreneurs.

Administration was everything for Simon, and his influence remains strong and pervasive throughout the business schools of today, where students learn Simonian administration and the tools, techniques, factors, methods, and processes to implement it. These students are then sent out to replicate these tools and methods in the business firms they join.

Michael Porter (1947–) introduced a greater focus on external market forces extending beyond internal managerial control. Managers should not only aim at controlling internal variables, but also analyze external forces and respond to them, and ideally shape them, in their strategic processes. Competitive strategy and strategic positioning became the new expressions of acute management insight and superior capability. Paralleling Chandler's use of corporate structure as a design tool for management organizations, Porter used industrial structure as an analytical tool for the establishment of what he called competitive advantage, an ideal of insulation, albeit partial and temporary, from the negative impacts of market forces, including competitive actions. Following Porter, managers could, like William F. Buckley in the political arena, stand athwart history yelling "Stop!" Strategic planning became the iconic vocation of MBA graduates.

Michael Hammer (1948–2008) added process control to the management control portfolio via the methods of business process reengineering, which quickly became identified by the acronym BPR. The core of the method was to identify all the processes at work in a company's operations, define the current state of these business processes in step-by-step detail, identify issues at that level of detail, and address them through micro-level re-design (or "change management") tools, which eventually took their own names, such as Lean and Six Sigma. One of the consequences of the reengineering movement was the use of mass layoffs from the workforce to cut costs in inefficient companies, giving this form of management practice a bad name in PR. Nevertheless, BPR and the concept of reengineering remain prominent in the management lexicon, suggesting the imagery of business firms as machines to be tuned and then run at high throughput levels under the control and direction of an engineer cohort.

John P. Kotter (1947–) proposed that leadership was the tool for change management (Kotter, 2012). In this context, management leadership is presented as a process rather than an exceptional attribute or characteristic, and anyone following the eight-step process can claim leadership. These managers establish the vision for change, set direction for action, and organize implementation. "Transformation" was a frequently used term for the results sought, implying great power for the managers who adopted the process.

The Management Paradigm in Practice

Paradigms solidify when they are associated with success. What we can identify today as the negative consequences of scientific management were disguised by the mid twentieth-century success of some iconic firms. The 1950s–1990s provided a unique economic context of industrial expansion and global dominance of American companies, despite any management inefficiencies. The United States had few global competitors immediately after World War II, when Germany and Japan were recovering and China had not yet industrialized. American corporations benefited from low global competition, rapid urbanization, and mass-market consumer demand, and not necessarily from superior management science.

Some firms used scientific management science effectively – for a time. General Electric, under both Reginald Jones and Jack Welch, applied rigorous efficiency-driven restructuring to boost short-term performance, but ultimately over-optimized and struggled in the long run.

GE CEO Jack Welch was lauded by *Harvard Business Review* as the greatest leader of his era (Fernandez-Araoz, 2020). One of the reasons he was praised was the reign of GE as the number one company in the world for five years, starting in 1993. In the world of management by objectives, the number one objective for CEOs of public companies was the stock price, total market value, and return to shareholders, and Jack Welch met his objectives. One of the tools was "earnings management": the consistent delivery on quarterly earnings growth targets and dividend payments. Welch assembled GE as a conglomerate through acquisitions, and built a division of GE, GE Capital, into a collection of financial assets (such as insurance companies) that held liquid assets that could be used, by moving and transferring them appropriately, to smooth quarterly earnings and confidently meet the expectations of the financial sector and so maintain stock prices (Hastings, 2024a). This practice was a form of "financial engineering," one example of the many levers of detailed control that were developed by the twentieth century's managerial specialists.

Similarly, IBM in its mainframe era benefited from scale efficiencies and appeared to master Porter's five forces, but only until new technologies undermined its monopolistic market conditions and exposed its rigid structure. Sears was an effective pioneer of structured retail operations but failed to adapt to the introduction of e-commerce.

Eventually, the management science icons toppled. GE suffered from over-management, bureaucracy, and a failure to innovate. The company's decline can be linked to rigid adherence to hierarchical structures and an overemphasis on efficiency metrics, hallmarks of scientific management (Schrager, 2019). The scientific method adopted by Jack Welch favored aggressive cost-cutting and divestitures of businesses that were not number one or number two in their industries. While initially successful, it eventually resulted in under-innovation and failure to respond to market change. The company's bureaucracy, installed to develop a special expertise in designing and enforcing scientific methods, hindered the company's adaptiveness and contributed to its downturn.

IBM nearly collapsed in the 1990s due to its slow response to the PC revolution. Inflexibility led to substantial losses. IBM required a cultural change, rather than a scientific one, in order to adopt a more decentralized and customer-focused approach and to eventually recover.

Scientific management worked in predictable, stable environments but collapsed in the face of technological change and competitive disruption. Scientific management appeared to be effective in a special economic era, but the constraints of lowered engagement and motivation, bureaucratic inefficiencies, frustrated creativity, and stifled adaptiveness led to the decline of once-dominant firms.

A Philosophical Problem

Hannah Arendt pondered the threat to humanism of the increasing drive to redesign and control the world through transformative science and technology (Arendt, 1958). For her, the main culprit is an idea – the idea that the world is objective. It's an alienating idea because it disengages us from reality, and creates an artificial world, stripped of humanistic concerns. With the objective approach, our businesses become objects like any other, reduced to data points to be managed, and they lose their civilizational potential. We engineer and transform them, and they lose their human value. The loss of agency and autonomy that are consequences of managerial control, and the devaluation of human qualities such as spontaneity, creativity, and judgment that is implied, are the inevitable outcomes of what Chandler called the managerial revolution.

But in business management, the mode of thinking we call *positivism* won the day. Business philosophy became associated with positivist ideas of identifying causality through scientific observation. There was an immense optimism that science would soon solve all business problems and that business technocrats would engineer a new and better world. It was not to be.

2 The Consequences of Managerial Systems

While Hanna Arendt was making an existential appeal about positivism in general, it is appropriate to draw some parallels between management practices and their consequences, and her critique of the modern drive to control the world through science and technology.

Bureaucratic Processes: Corporate bureaucracy and the widespread adoption of bureaucratic processes within organizations have been the inevitable consequences of the managerial approach to business. The management approach, the evolution of which we tracked in Section 1, emphasizes control. Formal rules and procedures, hierarchical structures, and clear lines of authority are designed and imposed to implement this control. People must implement the prescribed processes, subject themselves to the prescribed measurements, follow the rules, and be "loyal." Jobs are clearly defined in terms of rank, salary, and duties. In the pursuit of efficiency, specialization becomes narrower and narrower for each job, permitting the individual to use a limited range of their human abilities. People become subordinated and dependent.

The term *bureaucracy* is "always applied with an opprobrious connotation" (Mises, 1944). No one likes it. But because of managerialism, bureaucracy has become "the water in which we swim" (Graeber, 2015). Business has become accustomed to it. Sociologist Max Weber saw bureaucratic forms of organization as superior to any alternative form, indispensable for large firms and institutions, even though the inevitable result was to lock humanity in a joyless "iron cage." Robert K. Merton captured the problem (Merton, 1949) as bureaucratic dysfunction, a cause of social disruption rather than stability. It's a sad picture.

Heavy-handed Control: Management systems aim to eliminate variance from plans and forecasts and reduce outcome uncertainty as much as possible. Since variation and selection are normal conditions in markets, the extent of the control effort must be considerable to overcome them. Decision-making is centralized in the hands of senior management in pursuit of goals of uniformity and productivity. Henry Ford's management style at the Ford Motor Company established the uniformity norm early in the twentieth century, and, despite the high turnover rates and labor unrest that followed, Ford's methods were often imitated. Douglas McGregor (McGregor, 1985) called this management style "Theory X." It rests on the assumption that it is the nature of humans to be lazy and not very capable, and that management must be authoritarian and control-oriented to extract effort from them.

Performance Metrics: Use of Quantifiable Measures to Assess Performance and Productivity. The managerial revolution brought with it a focus on performance metrics, where managers relied heavily on quantifiable measures to evaluate productivity and efficiency. The obsession with quantification to the exclusion of qualitative evaluation represents the widespread adoption of Frederick Winslow Taylor's principles of scientific management, where time and motion studies were used to determine the "one best way" to perform tasks. Over time, this reliance on metrics evolved into complex systems of performance evaluation, such as the Balanced Scorecard developed by Robert S. Kaplan and David P. Norton (Kaplan, 1996), which expanded the focus beyond just financial measures to include customer satisfaction, internal processes, and innovation. While performance metrics have improved accountability and clarity, they have also been criticized for encouraging short-term thinking and neglecting human factors, as discussed in Michael Jensen's critique of performance measurement systems in his work on "agency theory" (Jensen, 1998).

The focus on what can be measured rather than what truly matters undermines qualitative judgment, intuition, experience, and the application of context-specific knowledge, which are vital to maintaining customer service standards and responsiveness. It can also create a culture of superficiality where employees seek out ways to game the system and never experience the joy and satisfaction of meaningful work. Ian McGilchrist (McGilchrist, 2019) sees quantification as part of Western society's left hemisphere–dominated analytical, logical, and reductionist approach that threatens the health of not just organizations but also the broader culture and civilization.

Standardization: Implementation of Standardized Practices and Policies across the Organization

Standardization became a hallmark of the managerial revolution, as companies sought to ensure consistency and efficiency across all operations. Standardization also extended to administrative functions, so that procedures such as budgeting, scheduling, and reporting often became formalized and rigid. The whole point of standardization was to bring about significant efficiencies and to limit flexibility and adaptability. When Japanese companies were the first to emphasize the need for systems to be adaptable and responsive to changes in the environment in order to achieve continuous improvement and enhance quality, Western companies encountered difficulties in shedding standardized practices. Toyota Production System workers could follow the practice of Jidoka to take prompt action to correct a problem at any point in the production process. Jidoka can be translated as automation with human wisdom (Turner, 2020), a nonstandardized mindset.

Professional Management: The managerial revolution elevated the role of professional managers, positioning them as experts and key figures in the achievement of organizational goals. This shift was notably articulated by Peter Drucker, who argued that management itself had become a crucial institution in society, responsible for the economic and social well-being of employees and the community. The rise of the MBA degree, pioneered by institutions like Harvard Business School, reflects this professionalization of management, training individuals to approach business problems with analytical rigor and strategic thinking. However, this professionalization also led to a separation between ownership and management, as explored by Berle and Means in "The Modern Corporation and Private Property," which highlighted the potential for conflicts of interest between managers, who control the day-to-day operations, and shareholders, who own the company.

Economist Ludwig von Mises wrote that the rise of managerialism and the managerial class undermined the fundamental principles of capitalism: "The capitalist system is not a managerial system; it is an entrepreneurial system" (Mises, 1998). For von Mises, the function of entrepreneurship is the determination of how and where to deploy capital, especially in new and innovative ways to meet customer needs. The execution of other details is left to the function of management. The managerial function is subservient to the entrepreneurial function. When scientific management overturns this relationship, the entrepreneurial driving force of the market system, with all its innovation and imaginative value creation, is reined in.

Stifling Creativity and Innovation: Overemphasis on Rules and Procedures Can Limit Flexibility and Discourage Creative Thinking

Managerialism often imposes rigid structures, standardized procedures, and strict adherence to established practices. While they were developed to ensure efficiency and consistency, they often resulted in stifled creativity and innovation. An example that is often cited is the Xerox Palo Alto Research Center (PARC) in the 1970s. PARC was responsible for groundbreaking innovations like the graphical user interface (GUI) and the computer mouse. However, the rigid corporate structure at Xerox failed to recognize and capitalize on these innovations, which were later successfully developed by companies like Apple and Microsoft. This illustrates how a focus on rules, procedures, and existing business models can cause organizations to miss out on potentially transformative ideas.

Clayton Christensen's concept of "The Innovator's Dilemma" (1997) further explores this issue, showing how successful companies often fail to innovate because their processes and structures are optimized for existing products and markets, making them resistant to disruptive innovations. The managerial focus on maintaining control and efficiency can lead to a risk-averse culture where employees are discouraged from taking the creative risks necessary for innovation.

Reducing Empathy and Employee Well-being: Focus on Metrics and Performance Can Lead to Neglect of the Human and Emotional Aspects of Management

The emphasis on quantifiable metrics in managerialism was belatedly understood to cause the neglect of the human aspects of management, such as empathy, employee well-being, and emotional intelligence. This became evident in so-called "high-pressure environments" where performance metrics dominated the organizational culture, such as in some financial services and tech companies. A case in point is the "Wells Fargo scandal" of 2016, where the bank's intense focus on numerical sales targets led to unethical behavior, including the creation of millions of fake accounts. The relentless pressure to meet sales goals, without regard for employee well-being or ethical considerations, fostered a toxic work environment and severely damaged the company's reputation.

Daniel Goleman's work on Emotional Intelligence (1995) emphasizes the importance of empathy, self-awareness, and social skills in leadership. He argues that these qualities are often undervalued in traditional management approaches that prioritize metrics over human relationships, and that the measurement focus leads not only to unhealthy work environments but also to poorer long-term organizational performance.

Centralization of Power: Concentration of Decision-making Power in the Hands of a Few Managers, Potentially Leading to a Disconnect with Lower-level Employees and Customers

A core tenet of the managerial revolution was to centralize corporate power, so that decision-making is concentrated at the top levels of the organization. This created a kind of management feudalism, a significant disconnect between senior managers and lower-level employees, as well as between the organization and its customers. An example of this is the decline of Kodak, once a dominant player in the photography industry. Kodak's management was slow to adapt to the digital revolution, partly because decision-making was highly centralized and insulated from the insights and innovations emerging at lower levels of the company. The leadership's focus on maintaining the status quo in film photography led to a failure to embrace digital technology, ultimately resulting in Kodak's bankruptcy in 2012.

The dangers of centralized power are also highlighted in Chris Argyris' work on Organizational Learning (1992). Argyris argues that centralized decision-making structures can hinder organizational learning by suppressing feedback from lower levels and discouraging open communication. This can lead to a lack of responsiveness to changes in the external environment and a failure to innovate or address emerging problems effectively.

Overall, the managerial emphasis on control, efficiency, and metrics has brought negative consequences for creativity, employee well-being, and organizational adaptability.

3 Shifting the Paradigm: Anomalies and Crisis

The control-focused approach to business management that dominated for most of the twentieth century represents a paradigm: the most broadly accepted philosophy of business management, the standard model to be followed by members of a community.

When Thomas Kuhn used the term paradigm in *The Structure of Scientific Revolutions*, his context was the scientific community, where the "accepted examples of scientific practice, including laws, theories, applications, experiment and instrumentation provide the models that create a coherent tradition and serve as the commitments which constitute a scientific community in the first place" (Hacking, 1962).

The concept of a paradigm is legitimately transferable to the management community, those academics, consultants, practitioners, and students who frame the philosophy and culture of business management and their cultural application.

Kuhn portrayed a paradigm shift (a scientific revolution, in his words) as a change in worldview, a new cognitive orientation, constituting progress from less adequate to more adequate conceptions of the world. Science advances by alternately constructing and destroying paradigms.

In Kuhn's view, a paradigm is all-encompassing, from a set of philosophical assumptions "at the top" to methods and tools "at the bottom." Between the top and the bottom are theories and some specific examples of solved problems, which are important components of the paradigm (Hillix & L'Abate, 2012). Kuhn calls them paradigmatic examples; we can equate them directly to case studies in business schools or consultant recipes for business success, or biographical histories published by business executives. In fact, Kuhn points to the role of specialized textbooks and history books in scientific disciplines as having the effect of rationalizing and glorifying the paradigm. Writers claim developments that lead to the "correct" paradigmatic view.

Readers and adherents develop great fondness for the paradigm. The paradigm is socioculturally constructed; the process is subjective, a system of values about how to perceive reality, a collective style of thinking (Guerra, Capitelli, & Longo, 2012).

The inclusive paradigm must demonstrate results and accomplishments to attract the allegiance of the majority of practitioners in the field. The paradigm must make clear predictions. Eventually, those nurtured within the paradigm come to accept it without much inquiry about the preconceptions that are involved.

As a consequence, the paradigm is not easily given up. When experience does not agree with expectations, the anomaly is shrugged off as an unimportant exception or error. This explains why, in the field of business management, we observe that traditional management practices and forms of organization are maintained even when the competitive marketplace demonstrates the disruptive power of new approaches.

But in Kuhn's construct, the anomalies become so frequent and so obvious that they can't be ignored. The paradigm enters "crisis" mode.

New practitioners, often younger than the paradigmatic loyalists, start to propose alternatives. Thy conduct some new experiments. Eventually they triumph by solving some of the problems posed by the anomalies. The new paradigm attracts new converts. It establishes new methods, new problems, and new language. The new paradigm will not solve all of the problems, and may introduce some new ones. The world is seen differently.

The Paradigm in Crisis

The consequences of the management paradigm become the anomalies of the Kuhnian framework – the unresolvable errors that undermine and ultimately collapse the system. Some of the anomalies of the type that Kuhn identified as leading to crisis are easily visible.

Centralized Authority and Hierarchy Control People but Not Outcomes

The hierarchy of authority is the foundational characteristic of the old paradigm. The standard organizational design is for a top-down, centralized authority structure, with a CEO, C-suite, and Board of Directors at the apex, supported by layered hierarchies of vice-presidents, executives, managers, and supervisors. Leadership and authority are tied to titles, which signify rank and decision-making power within a rigid chain of command. Leadership is framed as the exercise of vision-setting, decision-making, and directive-giving from the top, with the assumption that strategic insight resides at the apex. Job descriptions define what each individual must do in their daily work. The structure defines how power, decisions, and resources are distributed. It underpins all other elements, such as planning and management, and is a primary source of rigidity. The inherent assumption that strategic insight and competence reside at the top marginalizes lower-level contributions.

Hierarchical control systems were designed for a stable business world of relatively slow change. Anomalies arise as change accelerates in the economic ecosystem and rapid adaptation becomes needed. Decision-making bottlenecks occur, and frontline knowledge is ignored. The hierarchy fosters bureaucracy, slowing responsiveness in dynamic markets, as seen in cases like Kodak's slow response to digital photography. What seemed to be controllable becomes fragile and susceptible to disruption. The system becomes unstable because it can't adapt to external change fast enough.

The Mechanistic Production Model Fails in a World of Customer Primacy

The old-paradigm organization operates on an inside-out production model, which was originally designed to manufacture standardized products or services for consumption. The focus is on optimizing internal processes to maximize output, with customers positioned as recipients of what the organization produces. This production-centric mindset is a core driver of the paradigm, shaping strategy, segmentation, and resource allocation. It prioritizes efficiency over customer-centricity, which can prove to be a key limitation in today's customer-dominated markets.

This model assumes predictable demand and stable markets, but anomalies emerge when customer preferences shift rapidly or when customization is demanded (e.g., via digital platforms). The inside-out approach disconnects organizations from evolving customer needs, as seen in, for example, Blockbuster's failure to adapt to streaming (Davis, 2013).

The old paradigm is challenged by the new active role customers play in determining the flow of innovation from the outside in.

Top-Down Strategy and Competitive Positioning

Strategy is formulated centrally, focusing on competitive positioning within defined industry boundaries ("where to play, how to win"). It emphasizes market share, differentiation, or cost leadership, often benchmarked against rivals, with an aim to dominate specific market segments. Strategy sets the organization's direction and resource allocation, making it a high-influence characteristic. Its competitive, zero-sum focus shapes the organization's worldview.

This approach assumes stable industry structures and linear competition, but anomalies arise in disruptive environments where boundaries blur (e.g., Amazon entering healthcare). The focus on rivalry over collaboration or ecosystem-building limits adaptability, as Nokia experienced when its focus on dominating the mobile phone market blinded it to the smartphone ecosystem shift driven by Apple and Google.

Strategic planning can get in the way of the experimental action required for adaptation to changing markets. Modern tech companies are finding that a dynamic portfolio of experimental initiatives and projects, given time to mature into new businesses or new service offerings, gives better results than forward planning. They identify large profit pools across industries where multiple firms can be successful without fighting over market share. Alphabet's multiple revenue generation sources, ranging from internet search to media to self-driving cars, cloud computing, chips and AI, horizontally linked by AI and infrastructure, provides a contemporary example where competition for market share is not a highly relevant constraint.

Segmented Organizational Structure

The paradigmatic organization is divided into siloed units – departments, functions, regions, or business units – for control and specialization. Each segment operates with defined roles, budgets, and objectives, often competing internally for resources. Segmentation is a structural enabler of control, but significantly influences inefficiency and disconnection by increasing the organizational cost of cross-functional collaboration. Consequences include misaligned priorities and duplicated efforts.

In dynamic markets, silos struggle to integrate knowledge or respond holistically to customer needs, as we see with traditional automotive firms lagging in electric vehicle integration because siloed R&D and marketing functions struggle to align, delaying product innovation.

Organizational initiatives seek to address the silo problem through horizontal collaboration, flexible role descriptions and distributed functionality. But a full shift to a self-organizing network is prevented by the fundamentals of the hierarchical control orientation.

Centralized Planning and Target-Setting

The old paradigm organization relies on centralized, periodic planning cycles that produce detailed plans and numerical targets for all segments and individuals. Targets are often ambitious ("stretch goals"), tied to incentives for achievement and penalties for failure, driving performance evaluation.

Planning and targets operationalize strategy but their rigidity is a major source of anomalies. The planning approach assumes predictability and control over outcomes, but anomalies emerge in volatile environments where plans quickly become obsolete, or struggle to accommodate real-time shifts, such as supply chain disruptions. Stretch goals can also foster short-termism or unethical behavior, as with Wells Fargo's notorious fake accounts scandal (Witman, 2018).

Coercive Management and Supervision

The concept of management is constitutive for the control paradigm. Managers act as enforcers of plans and targets, wielding coercive authority to direct and monitor subordinates. Supervision aims to ensure compliance, with managers serving as gatekeepers of resources and performance evaluators. The model assumes managers have superior insight, but anomalies arise when frontline workers possess better contextual knowledge. Coercive management also demotivates employees, reducing engagement (e.g., Gallup's data on low and declining employee engagement in hierarchical firms (Harter, 2025)). Micromanagement stifles innovation, as seen in overly controlled R&D teams failing to match agile competitors.

The crisis for coercive management is highlighted by modern systems thinking. Complex systems are not responsive to management; their multiple realizability (i.e., many outcomes are equally probable and none are predictable with certainty) precludes it.

Performance Monitoring and Control

Data is collected to track progress against plans and targets, focusing on operational and market outcomes. Deviations trigger corrective actions, such as process adjustments or resource reallocation, to realign with goals. Monitoring is a feedback mechanism, less influential than strategy or structure but critical for maintaining control. Its reactive nature limits adaptability, because it prioritizes lagging indicators (e.g., sales) over leading indicators (e.g., customer sentiment), creating anomalies when market shifts are missed. Overreliance on quantitative metrics also ignores qualitative insights.

Suppression of Dissent and Enforced Alignment

The paradigmatic organization can discourage dissent, valuing alignment with centralized goals over debate or diversity of thought. Nonperformers or dissenters may be marginalized, disciplined, or removed to maintain cohesion. This cultural element reinforces control, but its stifling effect is a key anomaly. Suppressing dissent limits innovation and adaptability, as alternative perspectives are silenced. Anomalies arise when organizations fail to anticipate disruptions due to groupthink (e.g., GM's slow response to fuel efficiency trends). Whistleblowers exposing flaws are often ignored, delaying necessary change.

Mechanistic Change Management

Change is treated as a controlled process, managed through structured interventions like reorganizations, process reengineering, or strategic pivots. The organization is viewed as a machine that can be retuned or repaired to restore performance. In this model, change management is a reactive tool, less influential than core structural elements. Its mechanistic assumptions highlight the paradigm's limits. The assumption is that change is manageable and controllable, but anomalies emerge in complex, emergent environments where linear interventions fail (e.g., Sears' failed turnaround efforts). It also underestimates cultural and human factors.

Static Job Descriptions and Specialization

Roles and responsibilities tend to be rigidly defined in job descriptions, with employees assigned specialized tasks to maximize efficiency. Cross-functional flexibility is limited, and the job descriptions are tightly enforced. This characteristic reinforces segmentation and hierarchy, locking employees into narrow functions. While job specialization enhances efficiency in stable environments, it hinders innovation in dynamic ones, and creates anomalies when adaptability or interdisciplinary skills are needed. When high return on talent is required, job descriptions and job specialization requirements have the effect of lowering the return by narrowing the guardrails.

Short-Term Financial Focus

The model prioritizes short-term financial metrics, such as quarterly profits or stock price, often at the expense of long-term innovation or sustainability. Decisions are driven by metrics such as shareholder value maximization. This cultural and strategic element shapes planning and target-setting, amplifying anomalies that can undermine long-term resilience. Short-termism can discourage investment in R&D or employee development, as seen in firms cutting costs to meet earnings targets. Anomalies arise when long-term trends disrupt financial models, for example, when conventional automobile manufacturers mistimed the lifestyle switch to everyday affordable EV'S led by startup companies in China. One of the problems caused by this anomaly is the relatively short life of large corporations, as the short-term financial focus triumphs over innovation and idea creation (West, 2018).

A Narrow View of External Stakeholders

The paradigm prioritizes internal goals and shareholder interests over broader stakeholders, such as communities, suppliers, or the environment. External impacts are addressed only when legally or publicly mandated. This worldview underpins strategy and production, creating more anomalies as stakeholder expectations (e.g., corporate social responsibility) grow. Neglecting the broader stakeholder groups can lead to self-defeating reputational and regulatory risks. The paradigm's inward focus limits its ability to navigate complex ecosystems. The recent trend of consumer backlash against unhealthy ingredients provides an example of forcing food companies into defensive, reactive change.

A Kuhnian Framing of the Management Crisis

Thomas Kuhn's concept of anomalies – observations, discoveries, contradictions, or failures that cannot be explained or accommodated by the prevailing paradigm's "normal science" – provides the catalyst for a revolution. In the context of business management, anomalies are the mounting evidence of the old paradigm's inadequacies, which create a crisis that paves the way for a new worldview.

Collectively, these anomalies create a crisis, in Kuhnian terminology, by demonstrating that the control paradigm cannot address modern challenges of complexity, volatility, and expanded stakeholder demands. They erode confidence in "normal management science," pushing development toward a new paradigm.

However, in Kuhn's model, adherents do not renounce the paradigm that has led them into crisis. They defend it. They may make some ad hoc modifications to eliminate some anomalies and counterinstances that are particular sources of trouble, but they don't concede a new theory. In fact, it may be impossible for them to do so. "Normal management science" contains all the design possibilities, all the data, all the experiments and initiatives, and all the metrics. It also controls the incentives, including financial analyst and investor confidence, the politics of the corporate ladder, peer recognition, and board of directors' conservatism. The paradigmatic institutions of professorial papers in peer-reviewed journals, articles in the *Harvard Business Review*, business books and biographies, conferences, and corporate speaking engagements are all bounded within "normal science." The tools for breakout are unavailable inside the boundary.

To facilitate the change to the new paradigm, "extraordinary research" is called for. Two complementary sources of novelty are required: discovery and invention. Discovery refers to facts that were not known or recognized. Kuhn uses the discovery of oxygen as one of his examples. Discovery is a process, not an event, and takes time. Eventually, oxygen became an important part of the emergence of a new paradigm for chemistry.

The invention of new theories, rather than the discovery of new facts and concepts, usually results in far larger shifts in paradigms, in Kuhn's view. Novel theories demand more large-scale destruction of the existing paradigm and major shifts in techniques and practice. Copernicus wrote that the Ptolemaic system of astronomy that he proposed to replace had "created only a monster" (Kuhn, 1962). In the crisis of chemistry that preceded the discovery of oxygen, the existing phlogiston theory had to be abandoned because it did not align with, and could not explain, laboratory experience. A novel theory emerges only after a pronounced failure of the existing paradigm.

The management paradigm has a particularly difficult time generating new theory:

> "Business scholars tend to have a skepticism toward theory and theorizing. Many of them argue that there is 'too much' theorizing going on in the journals, apparently ignorant of the meaning and use of theory in social science. A field that collects and analyzes data but does not generate theory has accomplished nothing (other than a mass of data). As Ronald Coase once put it (about American institutionalists), 'Without a theory they had nothing to pass on except a mass of descriptive material waiting for a theory, or a fire.' This applies to business scholarship as much as to any other field."
>
> The problem with such theory skepticism is that it stands in the way of developing and adopting good theorizing practices, feeds resistance to refine and challenge the body of theory, and perpetuates a relative inability to recognize good and sound theory. (Bylund, 2022, Vol. 36, No. 2, 801–819)

The transition to the new paradigm is discontinuous: "a reconstruction of the field from new fundamentals, a reconstruction that changes some of the field's most elementary theoretical generalizations as well as many of its paradigm methods and applications." The transition requires "extraordinary research" and novel experiments conducted by pioneers and rebels willing to leave prior practice behind in the search for new discoveries and theories. This research and experimentation is accompanied by philosophical analysis as a device for unlocking the new riddles. There is a search for new assumptions. The new experiments take place in "a different world," with rules that are different from those of the old paradigm. The people and firms who work in the old paradigm are unable to see this new world, don't understand its new language, and are unable to make the shift.

4 A New Worldview: Self-organizing Systems

An opportunity for a shift in fundamental orientation toward a new worldview for business management is presented by the invention of complex systems theory.

The twentieth-century illusion was to represent the world around us in the form of mechanisms. Everything works as a machine, whether it's an atom or a leaf or a bridge or a human body or a firm. We try to bring more mechanical order so as to exercise control. In order to understand something, we model it as if it were a machine, and examine its parts and how they work together (Alexander, 1980). The mechanistic approach replaced the humanistic approach.

From George Whistler and Frederick Winslow Taylor onward, an important characteristic of twentieth-century business management theory and practice was the desire to be seen to be applying the tools and methods and objectivity of the natural sciences, and to bring precision, efficiency, and predictability to capitalism's processes. Some have called this "physics envy," or what F.A. Hayek, in his famous essay "The Pretence of Knowledge" referred to as "scientism," an application of scientific methods in inappropriate contexts.

The form of scientific method chosen by business was a kind of reductionism. Taylor favored breaking down complex tasks into smaller, repeatable actions that could be measured, optimized, and standardized. There was "one best way" to complete each task. Like physical objects, workers could be controlled, manipulated, and optimized within a closed system of production. This approach was extended by subsequent management thinkers who believed that business organizations could best be understood and directed through quantitative analysis and rational controls. The reductionist tendencies of classical physics were preferred to the dynamism of human behavior and creativity. Mathematical precision was a desirable goal.

Scientism extended to complex planning and forecasting models for financial outcomes and plan targets. Organizations were treated as mechanical systems to be fine-tuned with the right data inputs. Management relied on numbers and ratios to make decisions. Today, this reliance extends to so-called big data, machine learning, and the use of algorithms.

Interestingly, as management became increasingly captive to its physics envy, science itself began to move on from the classic mechanistic physics paradigm. In the second half of the twentieth century, systems theory and complexity science emerged, offering a new way to understand the world, one that recognized interconnectedness, interdependence, unpredictability, and emergent (i.e., unmanaged) properties of complex systems.

Complex systems consist of a large number of elements that interact in a rich, dynamic, nonlinear fashion constituted by the transfer of information between them, and specifically including feedback loops that stimulate further interactions between the elements. There is a constant flow of energy to maintain system organization, and it can never be in equilibrium; otherwise, it dies. Complex systems have a history; they evolve through time, and their past is co-responsible for their present behavior. Complexity emerges as a result of the patterns of interaction between the elements. Each element in the system is ignorant of the behavior of the system as a whole; it can only respond to local information over a short range (Cilliers, 1998).

Systems must grapple with a changing environment and respond appropriately, changing internally without the intervention of a designer, a process known as self-organization (Cilliers, 1998, p.10). In self-organization, "the whole notion of central control becomes suspect" (Cilliers, 1998, p.12). There can be no rigid program to shape the behavior of the system.

A business firm or corporation is a complex system. Complex systems analysis typically starts at the level of individual agents: elements or parts that are active. They can be individual people, individually identifiable teams in a multi-team organization, individual companies in an economy or industry, and other agentic elements. They interact through processes, rules, and methods that have important properties (sometimes called "affordances") that evoke certain behavior from agents. The critical point is that the agents are interconnected and interact with one another, as well as with other elements like customers or suppliers, or banks. They respond to feedback. They're influenced by their history, and system history is vitally important to individuals' understanding and sense of meaning. The way that they interact becomes the observed behavior of the entire system. It is the interactions that result in complex and unpredictable outcomes, even if each agent is merely adhering to a few simple rules (such as a sales incentive in the case of the Wells Fargo scandal (Witman, 2018)).

Systems scientists coined the term "emergence" to refer to these unpredictable outcomes. A result "emerges" from the collective efforts, insights, tendencies, preferences, and interactions between employees, departments, processes, customers, and external stakeholders. No one has a full view of the interactions or how the outcome happens, but it materializes nevertheless. There is no centralized command, and any attempt to impose one must fail.

Complex systems are dynamic, evolving over time without any management. The science identifies feedback loops as a critical aspect of system dynamism. When agents interact, they experience feedback from the system, whether positive or negative, encouraging them to continue or to change, that is, adapt. The continuous adaptation to feedback and the changing environment across all the interacting agents often leads to unpredicted and unpredictable results. Forecasting outcomes or prescribing definitive plans are unrealistic behaviors in this context.

The term "self-organizing" is applied to the emergence of structure and order in complex systems, without any central authority. The information on which agents base their interactions is local and immediate, and whatever structures emerge are the result of decentralized, bottom-up action.

Self-organization is a Kuhnian scientific revolution and paradigm shift. Ann Pendleton-Jullian put it this way:

> Pioneering scientists were astute enough to realize that the answers came from certain phenomena that did not fit known explanations, principally those that assumed top-down rules and organizing principles. Instead, they were all observing complex structures, forms and behaviors emerging from bottom-up, self-organizing interactions among different agents. This realization caused a fundamental shift in thinking, a shift so significant that it has revolutionized almost every domain. (Pendleton-Jullian, 2018)

Self-organization works because each agent in the system responds to its immediate environment – adapting behavior, learning from feedback, and influencing the behaviors of other agents. Over time, these local interactions accumulate and aggregate to form larger patterns (such as a business culture) that may be sustainable and repeated, while the system remains dynamic and continually changing. The self-organizing system can be both flexible and resilient. It draws on massive numbers of elements "rather than a single intelligent executive branch" (Pendleton-Jullian, 2018, p.170).

An example of self-organization in economics is the price system. There is no top-down management of the price system, yet a pattern emerges that integrates all economic activity at all levels. Knowledge of the relative scarcities of the means of production is dispersed throughout the economy, and the division of knowledge between individuals, without any individual having knowledge of the entire environment of economic conditions, facilitates final market prices through interaction (Hayek, 1948). A general solution emerges as a whole result of evolving exchanges, bargains, trades, side payments, agreements, compromises, and contracts (Buchanan, 1979). The system evolves toward a solution, even while the individuals who make up the system are struggling with discovery and understanding (Boettke, Caceres, & Martin, 2013).

Interaction as Capital

Interaction, between internal elements and with the external environment, is critical for self-organizing systems. Without interaction, self-organization cannot take place (Collier, 2004). The question of who should interact with whom, and when and how, becomes the challenge for the firm as a self-organizing complex adaptive system.

The industrial revolution metaphor of machines and linear processes that led to command and control, hierarchies, rules, plans, and goals as management ideals is no longer valid. Complex adaptive systems thinking is replacing traditional management thinking. Decentralization, perpetual novelty, adaptation, variety, and experimentation become the new perspectives. The dominant metaphor for firms as complex adaptive systems is exploration and exploitation (Axelrod, 2000), that is, experimenting and adapting on the way toward discovering new patterns of marketplace effectiveness, and then, once such a pattern tests well for repeatability, expanding its use until the effectiveness diminishes and a new pattern takes its place. This simultaneous explore *and* exploit capacity has been referred to as organizational ambidexterity (Tushman, 2013) and identified as one of the characteristics of breakaway growth in Silicon Valley companies (Steiber, 2024).

The mindset is humble, there is no attempt at prediction, and no seeking control. The dimensions are horizontal, not vertical, and the patterns are networks not hierarchies.

The primary variable for firms aiming to harness complexity is the nature of interactions and interaction patterns both within the firm and with the market and the environment – interaction as capital. All outcomes arise from the interactions of a system's agents with each other and with artifacts and with the environment. Just like physical and financial capital, interaction capital can deliver returns on the investments made in it. And, also just like physical and financial capital, interaction capital has a combination and recombination aspect resulting in new patterns that can lead to breakthrough differentiation.

Robert Putnam (Putnam, 1993) identified three emergent benefits of interaction capital: (1) generalized reciprocity – people enjoy working together, commit to helping each other, and place trust in one another; (2) trust becomes amplified as dense interaction rewards the cultivation of reputation by each individual agent; (3) a collaborative culture emerges as past successes at collaboration serve as a template for future collaboration.

Interactions Orchestrated by Constraints

In a firm that is a complex adaptive system, the interactions must find unity, a coordination pattern that constitutes a coherent systemwide dynamic and a distinctive interactional type. This coherence is realized through constraints – a term that systems scientists use to indicate not restriction or limitation, but channeling, guiding, and facilitating the energy in a system. Constraints can be cultural norms, ethical values, protocols mental models, conceptual frameworks, feedback loops, algorithms, and many more. Constraints can coexist in a variety of forms and dimensions; Alicia Juarrero introduced the idea of a *constraint regime* (Juarrero, 2023), a distinctive combination of constraints that can result in the emergence of novel properties. Every firm has a distinctive constraint regime.

Importantly, constraints are not causes, and they are not deterministic. But they do give shape to the possibility space of what can happen, what's likely to happen, and when it can happen. And they also shape the view of individuals located in that space – what they can see as possibilities. A system's events play out differently when constraints are different.

Therefore, in the new paradigm, it's important for a firm to be thoughtful about constraints. They can be classified into three types:

Constitutive Constraints: These define the essence and identity of the organization. They are foundational principles that give the organization its unique character and purpose and shape what it can become. They might include:

- *Core Values and Mission*: These give contours to the fundamental purpose and ethical foundation of the organization. They are guiding principles for the emergence of a company's culture, and they influence its strategic direction.
- *Organizational Framework*: Choosing a flat structure with defined departments and roles over a flat network shapes the interactions within the framework and is constitutive of how the company operates and its interaction capital.
- *Brand Identity*: A company's brand is not just a marketing artifact. It carries distinct characteristics including reputation, trust, image, and positioning in the market. These aspects are fundamental to how the company is perceived both internally and externally. These perceptions are important constraints affecting the firm's possibility space.

Strategic consistency, cultural integrity, and long-term vision stem from constitutive constraints, helping a firm stay true to its purpose while navigating changes and uncertainties.

Governing Constraints: These are the rules, norms, and limitations that stabilize the overall behavior of a system. In a business context, they are the regulatory, financial, and organizational policies that define the boundaries of the system within which a company operates. They maintain stability and ensure compliance. They might include budget limitations or rigid strategic objectives. Governing constraints ensure that a company adheres to legal standards, stays financially viable, and moves in a direction aligned with its long-term goals, but they can be stifling of innovation and adaptability.

Enabling Constraints: These are the facilitators of flexibility, innovation, and adaptation within the system. They can empower individuals and teams to explore new ideas and approaches, adjusting the explore–exploit balance. They can encourage creativity while maintaining coherence with the firm's overall purpose.

They can include degrees of decentralization, relaxed role descriptions, qualitative rather than quantitative assessments, innovation incubation, experimentation, and relaxation of risk management. Departments and teams can set their own project goals and respond to market changes and the results of experiments rapidly without bureaucratic reporting and approval requirements. Enabling constraints establish a safe environment for exploration, including acceptance of failure and error in the context of eventual success. Under the right enabling constraints, established processes can be modified, and new challenges or opportunities or newly identified customer needs can be addressed with new responses. The culture becomes one of enthusiasm for adaptability and continuous improvement.

The key is to establish a dynamic interplay – a constraint regime – where constitutive constraints provide foundational solidity and clarity of shared purpose, governing constraints provide dynamic stability for adaptive exploitation, and enabling constraints foster innovation.

Cohesion

Cohesion is the ideal state toward which a system of constraints evolves. Cohesion is the emergent unity of all system elements such that all their energy and mass are applied to the system's end or purpose, without any waste. Cohesion is dynamic not static, and not necessarily smooth, since external fluctuations and perturbations are unpredictable. For a business firm, the end is value creation, and cohesion is achieved when all the people and processes are applied to that end. A distinctive and sustained coherence is the essence of the differentiated firm that fits into an ecosystem in a distinctive manner to create new value.

The pathway to this desirable coherence is often unclear, since "management" is inapplicable; emergence can't be managed. That's why there is a dawning recognition that twentieth-century management orthodoxy has reached the limits of its usefulness. The goals of control, stability, and predictability are different from those of emergent cohesion, and are no longer appropriate. Dynamic innovation is the new target. Success emerges from adaptive, self-organizing systems whose possibility space is shaped, opened, and extended by means of distinctive constraint regimes. Constitutive constraints provide the foundational identity and values that anchor the organization; governing constraints set necessary boundaries to maintain coherence; and enabling constraints empower teams to innovate, adapt, and evolve within that framework. This shift toward evolving cohesive constraint regimes – rather than enforcing control – represents a fundamental evolution in business thinking. It makes possible a mix of innovation, rapid growth, adaptiveness, flexibility, resilience, and competitive differentiation in the face of complexity and uncertainty.

5 Pioneers and Experiments

The "extraordinary" initiatives to establish new paradigms, according to Kuhn, are conducted and led by extraordinary individuals, willing to work outside the normal guardrails in order to solve problems in new ways and to develop and explore new pathways not sanctioned by conventional authorities. Complexity theory gives them new permissions.

Complexity and its related concept of emergence provide the prospect of an ongoing, open-textured exploration of all possibilities. An expanding economy creates new economic niches for ever-newer goods and services through a process of experimentation and selection. Entrepreneurial firms conduct the experiments, and end users and consumers carry out the selection, thus sending signals for the persistent invention of still newer goods and services. The economy is self-constructing and ever evolving, without central direction. An economy is self-organized.

In this self-constructing evolution, experimenters play an especially important role. One of the observed patterns in evolution over time in complex systems is that the interaction of units or agents results in large numbers of combinations in a large number of configurations. Some configurations are more likely to be selected and to persist because they exhibit higher levels of what systems science calls function – they work better. There is a continual creation of new functionality capable of generating new value (Wong, 2023).

In organizational systems, such as the system of firms in an economy, we can observe new combinations and new configurations as they are created and watch them progress in the direction of advantaged function. As Kuhn predicted, they come from the fringes rather than the center. Organizational redesigns are particularly difficult. Starting from scratch with a new organizational value system has a better chance of successfully establishing and sustaining a new form.

The first examples of the new form's adoption started to appear in the second half of the twentieth century.

W. L. Gore: Management System Pioneers from Founding

The W.L. Gore corporation is a good embarkation point for a survey of some the innovators in organization. W.L. Gore was founded in 1958 by Bill and Vieve Gore, and has remained privately held. This is an important influence – the scrutiny of the public stock markets is often stifling for nonmainstream thinking about management and organization. From this position of freedom, W.L. Gore sought to challenge the prevailing paradigm of corporate bureaucracy and hierarchy by embracing a model of management that prioritizes autonomy (i.e., a release from control), trust (a release from command), and decentralization (a relaxation of the centralization of power). Over the decades, the company has become an exemplar of how a commitment to flat structures, small teams, and leadership through influence can foster creativity, employee satisfaction, and sustained innovation.

The Lattice Structure: A Departure from Hierarchy

W.L. Gore's lattice organizational structure is one of the company's most significant contributions to management theory. Rather than adhering to a traditional top-down hierarchy where authority flows from the top levels of management, Gore designed its organization to be flat and interconnected. In the lattice system, relationships are based on trust and mutual commitment rather than rigid authority, and communication flows freely across all levels of the organization. There are no fixed titles, no chains of command, and no formal ranks – employees, or "associates," are empowered to engage directly with one another and pursue projects and initiatives that align with their passions and expertise.

This structure encourages collaboration and autonomy, enabling associates to form fluid teams based on shared goals. Decision-making is decentralized, and authority is earned through influence and expertise rather than positional power. Leaders at Gore are often "chosen" by their peers, rising to positions of influence based on their ability to inspire and lead others rather than through traditional managerial promotion.

Small Teams, Big Innovation

W.L. Gore also pioneered "team science," with an emphasis on small teams. By keeping teams small and nimble, Gore creates environments where associates can form close bonds, innovate quickly, and adapt to changing conditions. Small teams foster a sense of ownership and accountability, as associates have a direct impact on the projects they work on and can see the tangible results of their efforts.

The company's commitment to small teams also supports its culture of continuous innovation. With fewer layers of bureaucracy to navigate and a strong emphasis on empowerment, associates are free to experiment, take risks, and develop new ideas. This freedom has led to breakthrough innovations, such as the invention of GORE-TEX, which transformed outdoor apparel and continues to set the standard for high-performance fabrics.

Leadership through Influence

Leadership has proven to be one of the most misbegotten concepts of traditional management science. The concept has been used to confirm and consolidate hierarchies of authority by claiming special attributes of character and charisma for those with power over others. At Gore, so-called leadership is not a position; it is a role that emerges based on an individual's ability to inspire and influence others in a specific context and based on a specific set of functional information applicable to that context. Associates at Gore do not have formal leadership positions, titles, or direct authority over others; instead, they lead by example, through collaboration, and by guiding teams toward common goals. This approach stands in deliberate contrast to the conventional management model, where authority and power are often expressed through rank and hierarchy.

The emphasis on leadership through influence cultivates a culture of shared responsibility and accountability. Associates are encouraged to take the initiative, make decisions, and drive projects forward, with the understanding that leadership is not confined to a few but can be practiced by anyone within the organization.

A Culture of Trust and Commitment

One of the most remarkable aspects of W.L. Gore's management philosophy is its deep commitment to fostering a culture of trust. The company's founders believed that people perform their best when they are trusted to do the right thing and given the freedom to act on their instincts. As a result, associates at Gore enjoy a high degree of autonomy in their work, supported by the belief that they will take responsibility for the outcomes of their actions.

This culture of trust has fostered loyalty and commitment among associates, many of whom spend decades at the company. They go the extra mile for the company. Success in retaining talent is a testament to the strength of a culture of valuing individuals for their contributions rather than their positions in a hierarchy. The lack of bureaucracy – meaning unnecessary layers of management and redundant roles – further enhances the sense of purpose and fulfilment that associates experience, knowing that their work is directly contributing to the company's success.

Avoidance of Corporate Bloat

The evidence seems to suggest that bureaucracy can creep up on corporations without explicit intent. W.L. Gore refers to this as "corporate bloat." In line with its philosophy of lean management, W.L. Gore has actively avoided the bureaucratic expansion that often plagues large corporations. By resisting the temptation to add layers of middle management, the company tries to remain agile and responsive to changing market conditions. Associates are empowered to self-organize around opportunities and challenges, without the need for approval from multiple layers of hierarchy.

The lean and flat lattice structure not only keeps operational costs low but also ensures that innovation remains at the heart of the organization. With fewer administrative burdens, associates can focus on what matters most – creating groundbreaking products and solutions that meet the needs of customers worldwide.

Legacy and Impact

W.L. Gore stands as a pioneering example in the post-managerial era of capitalism, demonstrating that a nontraditional approach to management and a decentralized nonhierarchical organizational design can be powerful drivers of innovation, employee satisfaction, and business success. The company's lattice structure, small teams, and leadership through influence have helped it maintain a culture of creativity and trust, even as it has grown into a global enterprise. Gore's success challenges the conventional wisdom that large organizations require hierarchies of authority and bureaucracy to function effectively. Instead, Gore's model demonstrates that autonomy, trust, and empowerment can lead to sustained innovation, agility, and long-term success.

Semco: Management System Innovation through Radical Transformation

W. L. Gore's founders determined on their pathway of innovation from scratch. Ricardo Semler inherited a family-owned manufacturing business, structured in the traditional hierarchical manner, with rigid rules, and top-down control. Semler approached management model innovation via the pathway of transformation. As with W.L. Gore, Semco's private ownership structure provided the new CEO with freedom to implement concepts that might meet with disapproval from stock market investors and financial institutions.

Solving the Problem That Traditional Management Created

Ricardo Semler started the journey of transformation from the perspective of a problem-solver:

"I was particularly distressed by the malaise that was all too apparent in our factories. Workers just didn't seem to care." (Maddux, 2014).

Observing a Kuhnian anomaly, Semler found workers unmotivated, disaffected, and disengaged. He felt a lifelessness and total lack of enthusiasm. Making matters worse, there were two philosophical camps in the corporation and, in one of them, managers were proponents of classical authoritarian solutions such as rigid controls and long, grueling hours. They felt that a controlling culture was necessary to get people to do their work. Workers were not to be trusted. Semler realized that the autocratic management style was wreaking havoc on the employees and the company.

The Vision to Break from Tradition

Semler had a radically different vision for the company than his predecessors, inspired by his belief in human potential. People must be trusted. Control must be relinquished. Trusting means sharing power and information, encouraging dissent, and celebrating what Semler thought of as workplace democracy.

One of his first actions was to dismantle the traditional hierarchy. He believed that most management structures were not only unnecessary to the success of the business, they also stifled creativity and innovation and so limited the business' potential. To relieve the bottleneck of concentrating decision-making power at the top, Semler introduced a model where authority and responsibility were pushed down to the workers themselves. Employees were encouraged to take ownership of their roles and empowered to make decisions that would traditionally fall to managers. This flattened structure challenged the prevailing norms of corporate governance and marked a shift in the direction of self-management.

Radical Innovations: Flexibility, Transparency, and Trust

Semler thought his goal of "workplace democracy" could be achieved through employee autonomy. Semco employees were given the power to set their own salaries, a policy that proved remarkably effective at fostering transparency and responsibility. Workers determined their compensation based on market rates, their contributions to the company, and the financial health of the business. Semler trusted that employees would set fair and reasonable salaries, and this trust was repaid with a culture of accountability.

Beyond compensation, Semco offered flexible work hours and workplace autonomy, allowing employees to set their own schedules and decide how and when they would complete their work. This flexibility was rooted in Semler's belief that employees were fully capable of managing their own time and responsibilities. As long as the work was done, when and where it happened was left to the discretion of the individual. This approach fostered increased job satisfaction, which in turn led to higher productivity and innovation.

A complementary cultural aspect of the model is radical transparency. All company financials are made available to employees, who are encouraged to understand the financial realities of the business and contribute from an informed perspective to decision-making processes. This level of transparency created a deep sense of trust and shared responsibility, which reinforced the democratic ethos of the organization.

Self-Organizing and Collective Responsibility

The most significant of Semler's innovations was to commit to principles of self-organization by moving in in the direction of what we will later call self-management. He empowered teams to make decisions collectively, without the need for managerial oversight. Employees selected their own leaders, evaluated one another, and were responsible for setting the direction of their work. This approach required a high degree of trust and communication and proved to be highly effective in fostering a sense of psychic ownership and commitment among employees.

One of the departments that were eliminated was Human Resources, reduced from ninety people to two. In its place, a new worker-led hiring system sprang up. Workers started to recruit new members for their own teams and fire those who did not measure up. Employees were encouraged to change teams, assignments, and departments regularly to broaden their experience and make themselves more valuable to the company.

Self-management at Semco was not simply a theoretical concept – it was deeply embedded in the day-to-day operations of the company. Workers took responsibility for their own tasks, but they also had a say in broader company strategies. Employee committees handled critical decisions such as hiring and budgeting, and workers were given a voice in the strategic direction of the company. This approach led to an organizational culture that was agile (before that term was fashionable), adaptive, and highly innovative. With decision-making power spread throughout the organization, Semco was able to respond quickly to changes in the market, new opportunities, and internal challenges.

Success through Trust and Empowerment

Semler was able to point to the company's results to support his organizational strategy. During Semler's tenure, Semco grew exponentially, expanding from a traditional manufacturing firm into a diverse company with interests in services, consulting, and technology. The company's workforce expanded, as did its revenues. More importantly, Semco became a model of a nonhierarchical approach to drive organizational success, creativity, and resilience.

Semco's success was a direct result of its decentralized, open style, which resulted in employees feeling genuinely invested in the company's success. Workers at Semco were not just cogs in a machine – they were active participants in the company's growth and innovation. This sense of ownership fostered loyalty, engagement, and a culture of continuous improvement.

Legacy and Influence

Semco's management innovations under Ricardo Semler have been shared via many books (including his own), journal articles, and case studies. Semco is a symbol of what is possible when businesses break away from the rigid, hierarchical structures of the past and embrace flexibility, trust, and employee empowerment.

Semler's legacy endures as a pioneer of post-managerial thinking, proving that organizations can succeed without the traditional command and control structure and methods. He has successfully transferred his concepts to businesses in hospitality, education, and financial services, as well as an NGO and a business association. "The principles I've used in education and hotels could only be identical to those used at Semco, because they relate to the manner in which people interact to make an organization move forward" (Maddux, 2024).

Haier: System Change through Destructuring and Entrepreneurship

One of the most direct challenges to the traditional command-and-control hierarchy of managerial layers is the case of Haier, originally a Chinese manufacturer of household appliances and now a multilayered global assembly of end-user experience ecosystems.

> Haier developed a networked enterprise, changing from a company that manufactured products to a platform that incubated entrepreneurs ... Haier gradually replaced departments with self-organized micro-enterprises, eliminating over 12,000 middle managers in the process. (Kanter, 2018)

The HBS Haier Case Study (#9–318–1040) quotes the CEO, Zhang Ruimin, as saying:

> A company is full of energy when it is small, but as it grows bigger, there will be more and more layers in the organizational structure, making the wall between the company and its customers thicker and thicker. The company gets more bureaucratic ... Employees do not know where users are. A finance staff is satisfied with receiving budget reports regularly. A production worker is only responsible for working on the production line. "Why do I need to care about users? I just do what my supervisor asks me to do."

Zhang set out to break structure. His Rendanheyi model is a platform rather than a structure. The first element of his vision is user experience, and he specifically refers to users (the "dan" in Rendanheyi) as distinct from customers. A customer may be viewed in the context of a transaction, whereas a user is seen through the lenses of continuous interaction and participation in the experience design and experience improvement process. Customers are lifelong friends who are close partners of all platform participants.

The second element of the vision is the micro-enterprise, a small and autonomous unit following market rules and, according to Zhang, "satisfying their desires by relying on their own efforts, instead of expecting the company to satisfy them."

The third element was the employee-turned-entrepreneur. Employees have the autonomy to know who their users are and to create value for them. Haier demonstrates belief in liberating the entrepreneurial talents of individuals as the driving force of company success.

The interaction capital in the Rendanheyi model is focused on user relationships, in that the ecosystem is intended to be interconnected through continuous interaction with user communities. Micro-enterprises engage with users throughout the entire value creation process, from product design, through production and delivery to the in-use experience. Through continuous interaction, micro-enterprises can encourage a population of lifetime users. As an example, one of the Haier micro-enterprises introduced the concept of the 'networked appliance," connecting its users to hundreds of food suppliers, giving those users an enhanced experience, and itself the opportunity for revenue sharing with the food suppliers. Product development is accelerated with user participation.

Haier provides initial start-up funding to micro-enterprises, as well as other resources (such as R&D services, purchasing, distribution, and the service network). In traditional business lines, Haier is often the largest shareholder of the micro-enterprises. The micro-enterprises can raise funds from outside VCs. Haier approves "user value creation" targets.

Platform owners (there were twenty platforms in five industries in 2018) set goals of market position and strategic pathways for their micro-enterprises, and provide incubation and growth driver services such as the Haier brand umbrella and distribution. They set the percentage of profits that the micro-enterprise owners can retain. Micro-enterprises aim to be the leading player in their industry with high value, high market share, and high profitability. They cultivate their user community in order to develop lifetime relationships and develop new revenue sources through new products and services.

Haier represents a complete repudiation of the tradition of building a structure of layers of employees working in divided functions to achieve objectives set for them by those higher up in the hierarchy. Instead of a structure, Haier aims for an ecosystem of shared knowledge, shared resources, and shared relationships. Instead of vertical layers, Haier aims for a decentralized network of small autonomous teams. Instead of employees, Haier aims to develop entrepreneurs. Instead of a linear management structure of orders passed from the top down, Haier adapts to nonlinear processes in which employee/entrepreneurs respond adaptively to changes in the market. Haier nurtures this entrepreneurship, and aims to empower everyone in the enterprise to function entrepreneurially. Instead of transacting with customers, Haier cultivates 'zero distance" to customers, meaning that they are an equal partner in innovation, service development and quality control, as well as a lifelong economic subscriber. And instead of paying employees for work, Haier cultivates the idea of pay-by-user – that compensation comes from customer value creation and user satisfaction.

Haier is an enterprise without boundaries. Its ecosystem approach replaces traditional value chains with communities of micro-enterprises that might include both Haier entrepreneurial micro-companies and third parties. All recognize they can create more value for customers working together rather than as competing individual entities. Smart contracts keep them bound together while also enabling bidding for new tasks when the value to end users can be raised to a higher standard.

One of the results of Haier's approach is the busting of bureaucracy. When there is an inter-enterprise service to be provided, a micro-enterprise comes into being to provide it, and is judged by partner microenterprises on the level of value that is provided. There is never a bureaucratic burden.

Valve: An Emerging Industry Nurtures Organizational Innovation

Organizational innovation has a long and successful track record in the video game industry.

A lot of new economic value has been generated in the video game industry in a short period of time. As evidence, video games surpass the global movie industry and global recorded music industry combined in revenue (Arora, 2023). Without a long history of corporate hierarchies and bureaucracy to shed, firms in this rapidly expanding industry embraced the organizational innovations of open source software, including anonymous collaboration among highly distributed self-organized teams, peer review systems, and agile processes.

In addition, the industry created its own laboratory for testing revolutionary organizational theories in virtual economies set in virtual worlds.

Valve is a company in the video game industry that pursued a value-generation logic to take organizational innovation to its logical conclusion: the end of hierarchy. The organizational design vision has been described as "a company that would attract the sort of people capable of doing the initial creative step, leave them free to do creative work and make them want to stay" (McCaffrey, 2021).

The design logic chain is as follows:

- Creativity is our core resource – the most important skill in game development.

- Creative employees are key to our capabilities.
- Creative people are most productive when left to express their own creativity in their own way.
- Hierarchy blocks creativity, as do planning and routine.
- How do we design a company to attract and retain the sort of people who are able to take the boldest creative steps?

The answer? Let employees decide what to work on. Let them exercise entrepreneurial judgment. Let them, in effect, do both strategy and implementation. Give them all the decision rights. Let them identify customer preferences – since they know the customer best; let them decide how best to address those preferences; let them decide how to achieve competitive differentiation; let them allocate resources, choose costs, and manage profitability; let them control quality and decide when software is ready to ship.

Employees at Valve work in self-organizing teams, and are free to migrate from team to team, and free to change their roles. There are no fixed job descriptions.

In place of command-and-control, a few simple rules or constraints have emerged for the exercise of governance. F.A. Hayek wrote about norms that emerge in social groups to shape behavior. These are not legislation, that is, written formal restrictions. They are what he called rules, constraints that everyone accepts in the shared commitment to collaboration and the pursuit of the most favorable outcomes.

The most significant of these rules at Valve is the "Rule of Three," a simple agreement that at least three individuals must agree on the initiation of a new project, or on other major decision points. The emergent standard was that this is just enough to prevent maverick behavior, and a low enough number to facilitate agile action that's not bureaucratically constrained.

Another rule or constraint goes by the name of Social Proof. This is a broader and looser peer review standard. If the original team wishes to recruit more members, they must persuade others of the value generating potential of the project (in competition with other projects in the firm); successfully doing so constitutes "social proof" of value.

Rules-Based Peer Review Process Replaces Management Structure

Conventional approaches to organizational design that we have reviewed so far often focus on structure. This might be command-and-control hierarchy, or structured networks, or strategic business units or functional departments. Valve abandoned structural thinking and replaced it with flow analysis. How can we attract the most creative people to our venture? How can we encourage the most productive flows of bold creative thinking? How can teams best assemble and collaborate for the most productive output? How can we integrate with the user community in the best way? How can the most value-generative projects attract the best resources?

These are all questions about flow. Economists in the tradition of the Austrian school are distinctive in viewing capital as a flow rather than a structure, and this view holds true for human capital just as much as physical capital. Emergent rules for self-organizing human systems can perform all the managerial functions that were historically left to control structures.

The new organizational insights emerging from Valve were (1) design organizations for flow not structure; (2) design to attract the most entrepreneurial people in the most entrepreneurial roles (self-selection); (3) let them self-organize; (4) let rules and value codes emerge; (5) treat teams as business units; (6) eliminate the boundaries between the firm and customers and other partners.

Unleashing Entrepreneurship within the Corporation

Valve's organizational innovation institutionalizes entrepreneurship and eschews hierarchical management. There is a particular focus not just on entrepreneurship as creative thinking and generating new business ideas, but on entrepreneurship as taking action. Entrepreneurship is an action-dominant logic. Valve grants employees the right to allocate company resources to their projects, and even to ship new games and features without consulting management or seeking approval.

While the ownership structure of Valve does not provide the employees with a full ownership share, the reward system encourages the entrepreneurial mindset. There is a peer review system in which every employee ranks every other employee from the projects in which they are involved together. The review covers skill, productivity, contribution to the product, and contribution to the team. Salaries and bonuses are adjusted by rank on the company-wide peer-review scale.

While Valve's revenue and profit information is not publicly available, it's reported to generate over $6 billion in revenues at high margin rates. The company's design for unleashing entrepreneurship is successful.

Buurtzorg: Self-Governing Nursing Teams

One of the most visible and most celebrated challenges to the traditional management model is Buurtzorg, a Dutch home healthcare company. It represents a pure form of what Haier refers to as zero distance to the customer. Customers, in Buurtzorg's case, are individuals who are at-home patients, often with complex conditions and multiple medical needs. Some of these needs require highly trained and certified nurses, and some can be provided by lesser trained personnel. The standard of care is often for multiple service providers to visit the home at different times to provide the different services, which can result in a loss of continuity of care and a disruption for the patient. Buurtzorg starts from the innovative proposition that one trained nurse can provide all the services for a single patient.

The operating unit is the self-governing nurse team. A recent report estimated that the Buurtzorg organization had around 15,000 nurses in teams of 10 – 12, with each team focused on a small neighborhood. Individuals in the team coordinate their own work schedules and loads, and teams confer with each other on experience sharing and emerging new knowledge. Teams exhibit minimal use of standard processes, allowing responsiveness to patients' unique situations in a context of holistic care.

There is no middle management layer. There is an IT system for online scheduling and documentation of nursing assessments, services, and billing. Coaches (not managers) are available to help problem solve for each team. A small back office handles administration. The mantra is: "How do you manage professionals? You don't!" (Gray & Sarnak, 2015).

Buurtzorg's performance has been highly audited by both government and private analysts. Patient-reported experiences are among the best of all home care agencies and its total costs are relatively low, even though its personnel costs (payments to nurses) are higher than average for the industry. Nurses report joy in their work, and turnover and burnout are relatively low (KPMG, 2015). Buurtzorg has experienced significant organic growth since its founding in 2006, driven by the effectiveness of its model of self-management and high-quality patient care and its positive reputation among patients and healthcare professionals. Buurtzorg continues to attract nurses and clients alike. Buurtzorg is expanding its influence in healthcare through consulting and helping other organizations to adopt similar principles.

FAVI and the Liberated Corporation

Terminology, or what some complex adaptive systems thinkers call languaging (i.e., an ongoing negotiating of meaning), is a difficult challenge for advocates of new organizational paradigms, because the old language is intransigent and consensus new language has not yet emerged. One initiative is to identify the adopters of the kind of radical de-management of the firm that we have been highlighting in this section as liberated firms (Gilbert, Teglborg, & Raulet-Croset, 2018). A liberated firm, or freedom-form firm, is "a company in which employees have complete freedom and responsibility to take the actions that they decide are best" (Getz, 2009).

Favi is a successful, growing French brass foundry. Its proprietary know-how in casting and machining of copper alloys was the basis for establishing its role as a supplier of automobile parts to car assembly and manufacturing plants in Europe and China. Favi is often cited as an exemplar of the liberated firm or F-form model. Favi actively eliminated hierarchical management levels and hierarchical control. The organizational unit is the self-managing team – called a mini-factory or mini-foundry in Favi's own terminology – in a leaderless environment where individuals take responsibilities for all their actions, from those that might be categorized as planning and budgeting (although there are no formal plans or budgets, and no planning department and no purchasing department) to design, manufacturing, delivery and customer service. All employees share four values: good sense, good faith (honesty), good humor and goodwill (Gilbert, Raulet-Croset, & Teglborg, 2021).

Teams consist of 15–35 people, and they operate independently; each has a customer, and individuals in teams act with complete freedom and responsibility to establish and maintain relationships, solve problems and keep commitments including on-time delivery and product excellence. Operators' autonomy and freedom are the cornerstone of the Favi system, to ensure that the worker makes real-time decisions to deliver the best quality to the customer on time: "the right part at the right time in the right place at the right price." Mini-factory teams know they don't work for a boss but for a customer.

The team can elect a "leader" if they choose to do so, but the leader remains an operative and returns to a production station. A 2009 paper stated that Favi had not missed a deadline in two decades and delivered millions of units per year without a single quality reject. The company successfully grows share in its markets, and achieves high margins and free cash flow.

Hierarchical control is replaced by empowerment and trust at Favi. Individual employees are trusted to set their own schedules, control quality and introduce innovation, meet customer needs and achieve the firm's mission. There are no job descriptions, no HR department, and virtually no rules or procedures other than those the teams agree upon among themselves. The shared mission is focused on customer satisfaction: "To be loved by all our clients." Individual employees identify what's right. Everybody is invited to contribute to the whole.

In a 2023 survey, the *Scandinavian Journal of Management* found that the term "liberated firm" was indicative of a movement toward the nonhierarchical self-management model. Under the umbrella of liberation, they included management models that have been called sociocracy, holocracy, spaghetti organizations, management 3.0, and teal organizations (El khoury, Jaouen, & Sammut, 2023). Empowerment, transparency, and autonomy for small teams are shared attributes of all these models, which are operated by hundreds of companies (El khoury, Jaouen, & Sammut, 2023). Oticon, SOL, IDEO, Quad Graphics, and Helios Technologies are among those often highlighted, in addition to Favi.

Summary: The Pioneers

The clear trend from W.L. Gore to the liberated corporation is the pioneering abandonment of the traditional methods and structures of command-and-control and the exploration of the new frontier of autonomy, freedom, cohesion, and flow. We will see that another independent vector, the evolution of technology, supports and amplifies the trend and opens up new possibilities.

6 The Emergent Novelty: Self-management

The foundational principle of management is command authority based on position, title, or decision rights. One company set out to abolish command authority completely, and thereby to establish the ultimate replacement for traditional management systems. The term that was used for this new approach was self-management.

Instead of thinking from the perspective of alternative organizational design, the founder of The Morning Star Company, Christopher Rufer, started from first principles. There were two: (1) there was to be no use of force in interpersonal relations and interactions in the company; (2) every colleague would keep their commitments to others and always do what they say they would do. These two principles constituted the entirety of the governance of the Morning Star Company for its startup mode. To quote Doug Kirkpatrick the Financial Controller and chronicler of Morning Star history, there were "no employee handbook and no giant rule book, no supervisors, no managers, no coordinators, no vice presidents, no titles of any kind" (Kirkpatrick, 2024a). There were also no employees. Every individual was designated a colleague – an elevation of status and an indicator of professionalism, and a clear opportunity for new kinds of interaction.

The New Language of Self-Management

The designation of individuals as colleagues rather than employees and the elimination of terms like "manager" and "supervisor" were more than merely cosmetic gestures. They were intentional actions that represented the new mindset of self-management. The language of the Morning Star culture was carefully and deliberately embedded in recruitment interviews, onboarding, orientation, training, education, and communication so that it guided people in a way of thinking about collaborative interaction. The language of HR in the traditional structures of management is intentionally dehumanizing.

The language of management locks in a fixed way of thinking. When managerial discourse reduces individuals to "resources," "assets," or "human capital," it frames employees as mere cogs in a machine, it subtly shifts the way that managers perceive and treat them. Words like "headcount," "productivity," and "efficiency" prioritize the mechanical over the human, stripping away empathy and individuality. Language shapes reality, and in this case, it limits the scope of humane and ethical management practices.

This mechanistic vocabulary can reinforce hierarchical, top-down power structures, where workers are seen as parts to optimize rather than people. As pointed out in critiques of workplace language, these power-laden terms make it easier to overlook well-being and creativity, favoring performance metrics and control. A shift in language – toward more humanizing, inclusive terms – can help create a workplace culture that values the whole person, not just their output. Most business leaders and managers are totally unaware of the degree to which they swim like fish in a vast sea of dehumanizing, acronym-laden workplace language.

The word "manage" originates from the French for handling and training horses (Kirkpatrick, 2024b). To manage is to have power over others. The concept of "human resources" is aligned with these power dynamics. As Henry Mintzberg put it: "A resource is a thing. I am a human being. I am not a human resource (Mintzberg, 2008)." The concept of empowerment, which permeated management language from the 1990s onward, is used in the sense of lending or temporarily granting power in a way that it can be revoked at any time. It does not dilute authoritative command and control. The Morning Star Company has worked very hard to eliminate power dynamics language from its vocabulary and to substitute the collaborative language of colleagues, agreement, and mutual commitment.

An Operating System for Individual Autonomy

The breakthrough for Morning Star, one that sets it apart from other experiments in decentralization, is the discovery of an operating system for individual autonomy. The operating system combines the first and second Morning Star principles (no coercion, always keep commitments) in a written peer agreement statement called the "Colleague Letter Of Understanding" or CLOU. These peer agreements are central to the concept of self-management, and in replacing the bureaucratic mechanisms of control and the politics of power positions with the integrity of voluntary interpersonal commitment. The CLOU is a statement of intent to act in concert with others. It's an accountability agreement between colleagues declaring each individual's personal commercial mission (why I work here), business process responsibilities (what I commit to do), scope of decision authority (what we both commit that I can decide), and performance measures (what I commit to deliver). CLOUs are negotiated not imposed.

A typical Morning Star colleague will have about six or seven CLOUs with the people with whom they collaborate the most in terms of time and attention. Specific responsibilities are identified in the form of a matrix that might include line items across planning, organizing, selecting, and coordinating, listing the pertinent colleagues in the network for each of these. CLOUs also include general commitments such as education and training and handling of proprietary information.

The CLOU provides the protocol for the self-management system. It enables the freedom for initiative, creativity, experimentation, and exploration with the responsibility of upholding commitments. It requires accountability and integrity in all individuals that others can count on. It supports adaptiveness and agility: CLOUs can be renegotiated and revised by mutual agreement when business conditions or the environment change, or new knowledge is acquired. All the CLOUs are interconnected to create a kind of collective super-intelligence that can be actively aggregated and tapped for problem solving and innovation.

One of the challenging questions regarding complex adaptive systems is whether or not they can be harnessed or guided or directed in any way, or can their self-organization proceed only in an autopoietic fashion. In fact, self-organization theory recognizes that global influence patterns can emerge from self-organizing entities that exhibit only a local interaction structure. Norms, consensus, and even leadership can be emergent properties of self-organization without being imposed from the top down (Puranam, 2025).

The CLOU represents an instance of this emergent self-governance. It provides the individual agents in the system, each of whom has an equal voice – that is, colleagues – with a tool to combine, via voluntary collaborative interaction, their individual intent with that of others to auto-generate shared intent and group action for value creation. Colleagues voluntarily agree about how they are going to interact with each other in their specific context.

The Replacement for the Organization Chart

The traditional organization chart, with its boxes, tiers, titles, and lines of reporting, visually represents the command-and-control mindset prevalent in hierarchical management. Each box symbolizes an individual's role and authority, with vertical lines reflecting the flow of orders from the top down, reinforcing a clear chain of command. The rigid structure implies that decision-making power is concentrated at the top, while workers at lower levels are tasked primarily with executing instructions. This framework emphasizes control, compliance, and uniformity, leaving little room for autonomy or decentralized decision-making.

This structure portrays the prioritization of authority and accountability over innovation and flexibility and the power dynamic that can stifle creativity and responsiveness. The charting itself and the associated negotiations consume time and work hours and involve a serious degree of people management and office politics.

The Morning Star Company never had an organization chart. Since the operating system for individual autonomy was based on CLOUs, there was no purpose for such a depiction of power relationships. At one point, the company submitted its currently existing CLOUs to a university computing facility in order to visually map the organizational form that Doug Kirkpatrick refers to as a three-dimensional dynamic network.

Figure 1 provides a snapshot of the web of interpersonal commitments for the development and operation of the company's first factory. The depiction is better viewed as a motion graphic (Kirkpatrick, 2018) which illustrates the

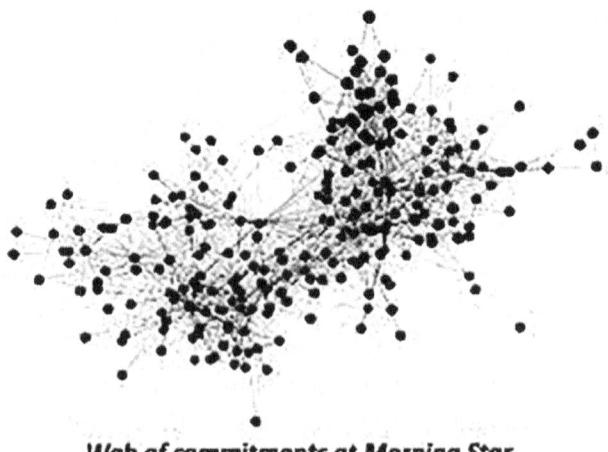

Web of commitments at Morning Star

Figure 1 Visualization of The Morning Star 3-dimensional dynamic network

rearranging and realigning of the roles and responsibilities of individuals and their CLOUs in the web of interaction as the needs of the business and its customers and the ecosystem change and the organization spontaneously adapts. People are free to enter or leave at any point, and the adaptation takes place without any command authority

The End of Planning, Budgeting, and Structure

Management is often an exercise in comparative statics. A starting point is identified, such as an annual plan. The metrics of this static point are defined in a snapshot of a current state, with all the line items and numbers of sales units and revenues, cost items, and derivative calculations of ratios and margins. The resources required to maintain and grow the state are identified, inventoried, and ordered. Departments are given their starting marching orders. A new, projected future static state is established in the form of the end-of-year targets. The required or desired progress is mapped proportionately from the opening state to the closing state, resulting in monthly budgets and targets and tracking.

Similarly, knowledge can become static, when it is tied up in departmental silos and not easily or quickly shared. Decision making can become a series of static points as proposals for decisions are handed up the hierarchy to higher and higher authority levels, where they are logged, shared horizontally, debated, and eventually, when resolved, handed back down layer by layer.

Budgeting and planning at The Morning Star Company are fluid and dynamic, and never static. There is no fixed budget. It's replaced by a dynamic cash flow model. The company has history of its revenues and costs, and they are expressed on a columnar spreadsheet. Interpolation of business history enables the projection of anticipated cash in and anticipated cash out by categories, and this cash flow is kept dynamically. There are none of the traditional variance analyses of why there's an expenditure in one category that's "over budget" or another that's "under budget." The dynamic cash flow model enables simulations of increases or decreases in costs or price or demand. Cash flow is a simulation tool rather than a control tool. Rigor is achieved by detailed monthly tracking over all the company's history from its founding, and projecting in detail up to five years, following every possible "what if" scenario.

Every month as the actuals come in they replace the projections and illuminate both the current position and future influences – for example, which costs got pushed into the future, which costs got eliminated, which new revenue streams popped up. Budgeting is redundant with this form of dynamic cash modeling.

Cash flow modeling is the apposite measurement for value creation. In the value cycle, customers express their value preferences in market exchanges when they pay cash to receive the benefits they desire from the supplier firm's value proposition. Cash is the mechanism of converting experience value into exchange value. Cash flow is the reward from the market for a value proposition that is well-designed, well-presented, and well-executed. Profit follows when the entrepreneurial firm chooses the right cost structure.

The unobstructed web of commitments created by CLOUs and the principle of no force releases even more flows. Knowledge flows freely from those who create it and process it to those who can use and it apply it. Decision-making flows freely because decisions can be based on the free-flowing knowledge by those with pre-negotiated and fully agreed decision rights. Bureaucracy, as we have noted, is replaced by commitments. Self-management eliminates the wastes and tensions and diversions of traditional management.

Summary

Self-management now has a 55-year track record at The Morning Star Company. The maturing of the digital age has integrated self-management into a new set of advanced organizational experiments.

7 The New Technologically Evolved Business Models of Hyper-personalization

Today, business management, as traditionally conceived, consists of decision-making related to planning, organizing, and controlling resources, including human, financial, and physical capital resources, to achieve business goals efficiently and effectively.

In the digital age, these decisions can be fully devolved to the machine (Lawrence, 2024) in a full integration of self-management and digital enablement.

The accelerating onset of digital enablement is changing how corporations are run and managed and even conceived. Digital enablement includes new capabilities and tools in multiple fields: artificial intelligence, process automation, analytics, machine learning, new networks (including blockchain), and augmented and immersive virtual reality. Digital enablement and the rapid evolution of business technology change our mental model of the firm from "the tools, the methods, processes and structures that we use as human beings to do together what we couldn't do alone" (Hamel, 2020) to a new model of digitally intelligent responsiveness to customer needs and wants.

The most fundamental effect of this change lies in the new business model that emerges from it, and compels a change in thinking about management. In this new digital-enabled world, the customer becomes directly connected to the firm and achieves new leverage in the business relationship. The customer truly becomes the boss in a different way than ever before. The customer experience – how the customer prefers to interact – becomes the first priority and the driver of all business variables, from production to finance to organization.

In a reinforcement of this business model shift, firms can now call upon artificial intelligence to mediate the customer experience. The new AI approach is to prioritize an understanding of how the customer prefers to interact. After profitability (which is the mandatory gateway – business can't proceed if it is not profitable), the quality of the customer's experience in an environment of digital responsiveness will be the number one attribute of business operations. Understanding the needs of the individual customer and interacting with those needs in the way that the individual customer likes best is the goal of the digitized capability. The essence of business operations, and the final shift from the mentality of mass production, mass distribution, and mass marketing, will be hyper-personalization.

Digital assistants and agents – a capability of AI – will become more closely attached to and associated with individuals and will sense their feelings – whether that's frustration with a process or delight with an experience. Businesses will build tools for empathic diagnosis, empathic response, and instant and dynamic updating. They'll become highly effective at hyper-personalization. In the new environment of high responsiveness, customers will exercise influence and control over their experience and through the adaptive dynamics of the digital assistant.

An example of this principle of customer-led commerce in action is 3D printing, which is the capacity for an individual to self-manufacture. The implementation of individual consumer desire is made materially operational, whether in the form of 3-D printed buildings, machines, or clothes, or food.

The governing factor is what consumers **feel** is appropriate to meet their needs and desires. They want instant access, fast and accurate personal request response, order completion and delivery, and complete transparency. They don't want the uneasy feeling of being tracked and surveilled. They don't want the diversion and interruption caused by sites selling consumer data to third parties to be monetized as digital advertising.

This consumer-led environment will require full personalization: understanding and delivering what each individual customer wants.

It's the opposite of the business model of the traditional management paradigm: mass marketing, mass production, and mass distribution. Examples of the new model are beginning to accumulate. A company like Nike is an early instance. It serves hundreds of millions of consumers. Its business is driven by what those customers want, when they want it, and how they want it. Nike's customers range from the very best performance athletes who want unrestricted performance at the cutting edge of technology, to more sedentary elders who appreciate comfort and stability. How can Nike serve all these customers with equal transparency? Via digitally enabled hyper-personalization. Every individual gets the experience they prefer and they design it themselves utilizing the services of a digital agent.

The Critical Capacities of Digitally Enabled Business Models

The digitally enabled firm uses digitization (including AI) to know its customers deeply (i.e., through data), fully understand its customers and their individual experiential needs (through deductive analytics), and meet those needs better than anyone in the world (through commercial engagement, operations and fulfillment, service delivery, continuous improvement, and innovation).

For customers in general, whether B2C or B2B, their experiential requirements are going to extend toward instant access and response that is both rapid and accurate. To become an effective consumerized or customer-led company, the digitally enabled firm applies technology and analysis to review, rearrange, and reprioritize its capacity in 5 core functions.

1. Branding and Marketing

Branding and marketing become the primary functions of the customer-led company simply because the first requirement is to accurately identify, deeply understand, listen to, reach, message, and persuade customers of the firm's value proposition. Without branding and marketing, there's no flow of information (and no flow of cash since marketing induces willingness to pay). Branding and marketing incorporate the firm's value proposition into customers' daily thought culture, aligning with and complementing their mindset and their perspectives, and shaping the firm's hyper-personalization capability. This marketing capacity is becoming hyper-automated since it is fueled by digital information flow, instantaneously processed for insights and driving the rapid reaction to generate the high-response relationship the customer seeks and, ultimately, the capacity to anticipate customer desires.

Branding and marketing are feedback-looped activities and the feedback loop lends itself to full automation without marketing management. AI can identify a wide range of human responses to marketing messages, from clicks on websites to pupil dilation when viewing video, and utilize these as triggers for the next round of adaptive and adjusted communications. Not much management intervention is required.

2. On-Demand Response Replaces Sales and Commerce

Conventional commerce, including e-commerce, will disappear as a management discipline as digital assistants become the power behind purchasing and daily life choices. They become dominant sales and commerce engines, to the digitally enabled firm's advantage in the case where they interact well with customers and integrate into customers' own systems and lifestyles. The result will be valued on-demand buying and delivery experiences and frictionless repeat purchases.

3. Order Fulfillment and Operations.

Real-time operational data and analytics will enable risk and error avoidance, predictive planning, and the scalable infrastructure required for frictionless operation. Fulfillment and operations provide the means to keep promises and meet expectations, two vitally important commitments in the consumer-led relationship. Amazon, for example, refers to its expertise in supply chain automation, balancing the demand for goods with the ability of manufacturers to produce them. Hundreds of millions of dollars in purchase decisions are made every week by machine intelligence in an ecosystem of automated decision-making. Machine intelligence is able to predict what human needs are going to be, make a delivery promise, and then intelligently adjust real-time variables to meet those needs with the best, fastest, lowest cost delivery experience for the customer. The machine intelligence is capable of "second-guessing" itself in reacting to circumstances – such as weather-affected delays – as they unfold. In the past, management would be appropriate for planning this process, but machine intelligence is superior in rapidly adapting it to new data.

4. Customer Experience Design

The customer's experience-in-use is the critical key to value creation, and the digitally enabled firm will be integrated into this experience, thereby opening up the opportunity for continuous addition of new and supplemental value and ever-strengthening sticky relationships. Continuing engagement after a purchase and after a usage experience is important. Some brands have created digital online spaces and experiences where customers can participate and engage, such as Gucci's Vault on Discord (Roy, 2023). Even when they are not buying or consuming, customers can be digitally engaged with their brands, without a management-directed active engagement process.

The critical capacity is to be able to design the customer experience. This requires a highly evolved empathy for the customer, not just in the context of their usage of the product or service, but across their entire life system.

5. Service Delivery Management
Process automation ensures delivery excellence and consistency, and customer transparency generates confidence and trust across all channels. Digital integration enables continuous improvement of processes whenever feedback indicates an opportunity. Digitally enabled firms exhibit excellent governance of the service experience. As digital service provision gets better and better, it will become a subject of monitoring but not management.

Organizing the Digitally Enabled Firm

How will firms shape the kind of digital organizations that are implied by these developments, where decision-making must be near-instant and the accuracy of a millisecond decision is so critical? It will be futile and dangerous to rely on traditional management styles. Leadership and governance will exist, but they'll change considerably. David Kramer, a founder of Co-operative Computing and a designer of digitally enabled business organizations, encourages us to add to our mental model the concept of a digital sapiens (intelligent AI agents) that work alongside *Homo sapiens* in teams (Hastings, 2024b). One of those digital sapiens will, eventually, be the digital CEO, connected to all aspects of all decision-making processes, governing in millisecond transaction times.

Firms will digitize across four dimensions.

1. Digitize **organizational structure**: There will be no place for hierarchy, planning, and command-and-control or any residual obstacles to the free flow of digital implementation of job functions wherever appropriate.
2. **Methods, procedures, and routines**: Where they have emerged and proven useful, they will be digitized for continuity and consistency. And when it becomes clear they need to work differently they'll be digitally reengineered for improved functionality.
3. **Systems and technology**. IT systems will increasingly facilitate people (when not replacing them), processes, and change. They will obviate any need for management.
4. **Key performance indicators**. Revised signals of success will be established with new measurements, monitoring, and distribution for action. The key here is not KPIs as control mechanisms (which is how they are traditionally used) but as feedback loops: building up an understanding of the current state and the patterns of its dynamics through data, analytics, and the response environment.

A current state of these dimensions is established not through management but through discovery, from which a delta is derived: what is required to improve and accelerate:

* To grow revenue.
* To become more operationally efficient.
* To continuously improve the performance of the firm through digitization and data-driven decision-making.
* To develop the cultural identity that best facilitates the collaboration of digital sapiens and *Homo sapiens*. There will be a different way of working and different forms of collaboration, and the cultural identity of the firm will be highly relevant to the nature of the adoption of these new ways.

Speed of Change and the Art of Possible

The acceleration of the rate of speed of change has been identified as a challenge for firms, but in the new customer-led digital age, the acceleration is in the hands of the customer. When what customers want is more and more attainable, they will learn to ask systems for what they want and the system will understand enough of what's available from all potential sources to recommend and bring it to that customer. The system will assemble sub-components into a solution. For example, if a customer wants a mirror with a digital camera in it and an audio source of weather information, powered by DC because they live in Denmark, and that particular configuration is not currently offered, a digital assistant will specify it from available parts and build a personalized SKU, deliverable two days from now at a specific price. That's the art of possible: not what exists now, but what it is possible to assemble quickly.

Asking the Right Questions

What is the role of management? The future lies in getting better at prompting: asking the AI the right questions: Can I do this now? What is possible? The questioner dreams it up, and the system assembles the dream. Then, the organization implements the assembled solution in the firm's environment and in the marketplace.

Copilot is a good early example of what's possible – a tool that observes and takes information and comes back to say, "Here are the activities at which the firm is not efficient that could be done much more efficiently." For example, the AI detects that people are keying-in data, and the process could be automated. It provides the art of possible. It could do the same for customers and customer interactions.

Constructing the Firm for the New Environment

Today's construct of the firm integrates the empathetic component (how do we create valued experiences for the customer?), the technical component (what do we need from a technical perspective to meet customer expectations?), and the financial component (how do we operate profitably and efficiently?)

Ask these questions of an AI and, ultimately, the AI will respond with a highly accurate recommendation of what company or brand to build. It has the universe of knowledge at its fingertips, with all customer and buyer data to reveal preferences and trends and desires. The best entrepreneurs will be the ones asking the right questions, while the operation of that business can be left more and more to the AI and the digitized firm. The AI will build a digital CEO that can develop a market analysis and a business plan, perhaps raise capital against that plan, sign up the initial customers, design the products and aesthetics, and the customer experience. Over time, the digital sapiens species footprint will expand, and the *Homo sapiens* species footprint becomes more specialized and focused. Competition will boil down to building specialized digital CEOs. The software might be open source and free, and the data proprietary, so the added value is in designing better digital CEOs from better data sets.

How? By asking better questions. McKinsey, for example, has decades of data and intelligence about good decision-making and what's associated with it. That could be the input data for building a digital CEO. WPP has data about great marketing campaigns and great marketing agencies and could create great marketing CEOs. Digital doctors will outperform nondigital doctors because of the mass of data around medical history, practice, research, and so on.

Management will become less and less relevant because digital sapiens can do more and more of it. Entrepreneurship – creatively asking the right questions and imagining the future in a better way than others – will become more and more relevant.

8 The New Integration of Self-management and Digital Enablement

How does individual autonomy scale? How do digital systems harness human creativity and the empathic interaction of value proposition design and customer needs that generate new patterns of human emotional well-being? We are beginning to see the emergence of new digital ecosystems guided by the energy of empathy in the development of commercial initiatives where autonomy, not management, provides the direction.

Handu Group in China provides an example of this new direction, which is distinctly different from the Western model of management. Autonomous teams operate within an internal entrepreneurship model, with direct access to corporate resources and capabilities. In full entrepreneurial mode, they self-organize around specific business opportunities without resort to management intervention, permission, or control.

In the Handu system, teams are responsible for identifying customers, markets, and business and innovation opportunities. A team has a minimum of three members: a designer in charge of product development, a web-page specialist responsible for online portal design, display, and sales, and a product management specialist in charge of sourcing, production, inventory, and logistics (Greeven, Xin, & Yip, 2023). As marketplace success directs, the team size can grow and new specialists can be recruited to add to team capabilities. The team monitors customer needs and value experiences, and autonomously adapts and expands product development, new product launches, discounts, and promotions. As products and sub-brands are added, teams are free to add upstream and downstream partners (e.g., specialized manufacturers who might be outside the Handu Group) to the ecosystem for customized production and distribution.

There are shared success indicators that guide all teams (such as sales, gross profit, inventory turns), but each team behaves independently in the choices it makes in responding to these indicators. The indicator dashboard is visible to all teams in real time, so that internal peer emulation norms evolve as a catalyst for achieving better and better results.

When the indicator dashboard shows subpar results, declines, or losses, the team will lose access to resources and may be closed down, with individuals transferred to new teams or new roles. Full entrepreneurial mode is equally as efficient in reallocating investment away from failing value propositions as it is in fueling the success of winning propositions.

Horizontal, Not Vertical

In contrast to the traditionally vertically organized hierarchical structures of the standard corporation, the new digital ecosystem firms are organized horizontally. The autonomous teams directly connected to the customer and to partners and suppliers via their digital commerce platforms constitute the front end of the horizontal structure.

At the back end are the capital assets to support the value flow to the customer that's orchestrated by the front end teams: production plants, warehouses, some computing hardware, and critical digital assets such as databases, including 500 different curated fan groups with over several hundred thousand fans in each group giving front end teams access to billions of impressions annually (Handu's Journey To Success, 2024).

In between, there is a middle layer of software systems that link the front end to the back end in providing the dynamic and adaptive capabilities for channeling demand, managing the supply chain, utilizing capital, and enabling the value experience. The middle layer is the internal digital platform that replaces middle management and organizes shared services, data, analytics, reporting, and the capabilities to assist front end teams in their rapid, permissionless decision-making. Middle-layer systems include business intelligence, warehouse management system, transport management system, supply chain management, supplier regulation management, and additional advanced service and management technologies. Every individual and every team can access the software and data they need through the same platform, which also keeps track of project activities, progress, and results. In a recent promotion (the "double-11" promotion celebrating China's Singles Day on November 11), Handu's processing speed reached 15,000 orders per minute. Individual teams can be confident of the processing efficiency behind them, supporting them in out-of-the-ordinary service and experience promises to customers

Alibaba is another Chinese company that has worked long and hard at perfecting the three-part horizontal structure. *Harvard Business Review* (Handu's Journey To Success, 2024) reports:

> Alibaba has perhaps gone the furthest in perfecting its middle: Its organizational structure centers on *zhongtai*, a digital middle office ...The digital platform is maintained and developed by cross-functional teams, not traditional IT teams, which helps ensure that it is responsive to the needs of more than 2 million merchants in hundreds of businesses and dozens of sectors. It is linked to Alibaba's complementors: third party payment (Alipay), cloud service (AlibabaCloud), logistics (Cainiao), and communication (DingTalk), among others.
>
> As a result, Alibaba's business ecosystem has become a data-driven, well-oiled machine of transactions and information exchange.

The HBR authors note that this middle is the opposite of static, designed to give the front end of the business maximum flexibility to change and evolve as circumstances, the environment and customers change.

The Efficiency of Project Focus

Another beneficial result of the autonomous team organization is the faster execution and decision making that emerges from narrowly and clearly defined tasks, timelines, and budgets. The small front-end teams in Handu are highly focused on their interactions with their own customer set on their own website, on their own line of products, and on their own indicators of sales revenues, margins, and turnover. There are no distractions brought on by central planning requirements, internal processes, meetings with management, or any of the usual bureaucratic impediments. Teams are incentivized based on their individual performance, with clear benchmarks to guide them. The feedback loop between customers and teams is immediate, and data on purchasing patterns and customer preferences can be integrated directly into daily decisions. Real-time data is used to modify product designs and marketing strategies, with instant response from the middle layer and the reliable support of the back-end components.

Digitally Enhanced Growth

Since its founding in 2006, Handu Group has shown significant financial growth, reaching over $2 billion in revenues. Initially targeting young female fashion shoppers, it has generated multiple sub-brands targeting different demographics, including men's fashion, children's wear, and middle-aged women's clothes. It has also become a B2B service platform, managing other companies' brands through its "management agency" business. The agile, data-driven, digitally enabled three-system model shows signs of very broad applicability.

The Case of Deepseek and AI

In early 2025, the Chinese AI firm called Deepseek unveiled its latest model. The Western technology community debated whether the new model and its low-cost/reduced computing power usage represented a new frontier. The consensus opinion was no – it represents some surprising advances in the quality of output achieved relative to the cost of development and what the AI community calls "training," but hadn't reached a new performance frontier.

However, Deepseek may have represented a breakthrough innovation on a different and possibly more important frontier, that of organizational design. The Deepseek model was developed by a business unit with no management and no business administration, no resource allocation methods, no levels and no hierarchy, no structure, no fixed roles, no titles and no politicized competition to climb the corporate ladder, no KPI's, and no targets. All of the traditional trappings of Western business administration had been thrown out.

This suggests that there is a new frontier of innovation, that of organizational design and business management.

Deepseek's replacements for administration are manifold and represent a completely new system (Yong, 2025).

Freedom: In place of business administration, Deepseek's founder speaks of freedom – freedom to pursue exceptional accomplishment. This is an enabling incentive for individuals, teams, and the firm. No one can plan in advance where this freedom will lead. There is only the beacon of exceptional accomplishment to aim for, without any false quantification of what that might be. Will people be happy with what they accomplish? Freedom enables them to find out.

Spontaneous division of labor: How is freedom organized? It isn't. At Deepseek, there is a spontaneous division of labor in which individuals create ideas, teams form and unform in developing those ideas, cross-team collaboration occurs as it's prompted by the evolution of ideas. Individuals are recruited to teams or they migrate to a team that they're aligned with. There's no HR Department, no job description, no bosses with instructions on how and where and when to work and with whom.

Discovery versus targets: The traditional Western form of management includes the setting of targets against which to measure outcomes. Individuals are given targets, teams are given targets, firms set annual targets. Deepseek eschews this form of management. The alternative to plans and targets is mission-driven discovery. The mission is AGI, the pathway to it is uncertain and unmapped, and the method of progress is idea-inspired experimentation to discover possible next steps. Discovery is action-driven, not target-driven.

Teams form around ideas: Teams have become a central tenet of advanced organization, built on a project management mindset. Teams are assembled around project goals, with the expertise to address identified project needs and the goal of completing the project. Deepseek assembles teams around ideas. Any individual can originate an idea and the team assembles around exploration and experimentation to discover where the idea might lead. It might lead nowhere, in which case the team can reassemble around another idea, or it might lead somewhere unexpected, in which case the team can reconfigure. Teams can collaborate across boundaries, so a team is not an exclusive concept but a self-assembling stream of expertise that can flow in multiple directions.

Transparency and knowledge-sharing: Conventional management concepts assume that specialized knowledge can and should be held and focused in departments, areas of expertise, or dedicated projects. At Deepseek, the preference is for total transparency and unfettered knowledge sharing. Every individual has access to all the firm's knowledge without restriction.

Resources versus resourcefulness: One of the traditional tasks of management is resource allocation – deciding who gets to utilize the firm's resources. At Deepseek, every individual and team has access to the firm's resources, without permission or planning required. An idea can command the GPU's and compute time needed to validate it. The productivity variable then shifts to resourcefulness versus resources.

Eliminate the politics of competition: To "climb the corporate ladder" in a Western corporation is to engage in a political competition with peers to gain recognition, assert superiority, and to individually break away from the pack. The Deepseek model – and perhaps the Chinese model – is to aim for collective effort and collective impact. The collective wins via exceptional achievement in a context of mission alignment and shared purpose. Teams share insights openly in order to accelerate innovation for the group as a whole.

Passion over experience: Deepseek founder Liang Wenfeng has indicated a preference for youthful passion over experience, whereas the latter is usually key to hiring preferences in traditional management. Experience, he says, brings baggage that can weigh heavily on open-ended exploration. For short-term goals, hiring experienced individuals makes sense. But long-term success does not depend on past experiences. Rather, it depends more on foundational skills, creativity, and passion.

In Liang Wenfeng's view, organization is not just an innovation frontier, it's the ultimate source of competitive advantage. He said, "In disruptive tech, closed-source moats are fleeting. Our real moat lies in our team's growth – accumulating know-how, fostering an innovative culture."

There is evidence that companies in China and other countries are not just loosening management structures but actively removing the machinery of corporate control at the firm level. Employees and teams are able to operate with a great degree of self-governance. Without a formal vision or mission, there is no leadership-imposed strategy. Instead of a process of top-down approval for resource allocation, there is a process of entrepreneurial bidding to support proposed projects for future value creation. The introduction of market-like systems, voluntary and highly flexible collaboration, and reputation and trust over authority represent a radical departure from traditional management. We could describe them as an organizational design innovation that is "post-managerial."

9 Enabling Cohesion: More Freedom, Less Authority

In Thomas Kuhn's framework of scientific revolutions (Kuhn, 1962) the changing tides of theory, method, and practice in a community are designated as paradigm shifts. Progress in thinking and doing does not occur gradually but through disruptive shifts when an existing paradigm is replaced by a new one due to anomalies and contradictions that the old one can't explain.

Management as a concept, and managerialism as its practice, is at the point of paradigm shift. Kuhn points to technical breakdown as the core of the crisis that precipitates a paradigm shift, and for traditional management, the technical breakdown lies in its central and fundamental concern, that of control.

The original goal was control of the battlefield and subordinated populations for the Prussian army. For George Whistler, the goal was control of outcomes so that railroad accidents would not happen, or would happen more infrequently in the future. Frederick W Taylor aimed at control of people and their work practices, for the purpose of "greater national efficiency." The centrality of control of both people and outcomes in the paradigm of managerialism has been maintained since then.

The mechanism for the attempted imposition of control is power. Power is exerted through hierarchy (individuals at the top of the hierarchical pyramid exert power over those further down), title (managers are the bosses of workers, and vice-presidents are the bosses of managers, and C-Suite executives are the bosses of vice-presidents), authority (the privilege of some to give instructions to others), decision rights (the roles assigned to some to make decisions that others must follow), resource allocations (control over budgets, and over project plans and teams), and access to knowledge (restricted circulation of documents and data). Management is practiced and implemented through power relations, underpinned by the belief that this is the only route to organizational coherence.

The rapid development of complex adaptive systems (CAS) theory and the concept of system cohesion through dynamic interweaving of multiple constraints provide the basis for the Kuhnian paradigm shift. CAS changes the dominant systems logic from linear causality to coherence. As Alicia Juarrero puts it, something "went wrong with these two notions" and we need to reimagine a different interpretive framework (Juarrero, 2023).

The alternative framework, the one that will constitute the post-managerial era, lies not in power and control of firms as systems, but in encouraging cohesion by adding increasing degrees of freedom that unleash the emergence of value. Freedom is the necessary underpinning for the new organizational model that's appropriate for the modern digitally enabled firm. The new model is a cohesive dynamic, a flow state, as opposed to a control process. The relentless requirement for change, adaptation, and dynamic flexibility that is characteristic of the twenty-first century requires the broadest possible range of degrees of freedom. Flowing freely requires freedom to change.

Organizational Cohesion

The new organizational design framework represents a complete departure from the historical hierarchical, divisionalized, central command-and-control structure.(Beliczky, 2025)

Dynamic Coherence

Whereas the traditional managerial structure aims at stability and persistence, the new context of business in the age of informational abundance is adaptability to a rapidly changing external environment of new technologies, new markets, and new customer preferences. Dynamic cohesion is a term to represent an organization's ability to remain in continuous motion, constantly adapting and evolving in response to internal and external stimuli. Dynamic cohesion ensures that organizations do not remain static or rigid but instead can pivot, evolve, and grow as market changes, customer needs, and technologies shift.

The concept of cohesion is essential to maintaining the dynamism needed for success in the twenty-first century because it governs an organization's capacity for change – not just reactive but evolving. Dynamically coherent organizations are designed to anticipate change, and maintain forward direction whatever the buffetings of the environment; they "hang together" in a unique way.

Dynamic design borrows significantly from biology. Just as a biological system adapts and evolves to survive in fluctuating conditions, a dynamically coherent organization constantly adjusts to new realities. Organizational evolution can embrace innovating new products or services, reshaping internal processes, or adopting cutting-edge technologies, with a combination of foresight and experimentation, utilizing real-time data and feedback loops rather than simply reacting to shifts in the marketplace. Innovation, creativity, and resilience are not only possible but expected. This approach enables organizations to stay competitive, consistently evolving, and maintaining long-term success despite external challenges and disruptions.

Netflix's content recommendation algorithm provides an example of organizational dynamics in action. It provides an adaptive intelligence system that continuously absorbs customer behavior data and refines Netflix's engagement strategies in real time. Rather than relying on static categories or pre-set preferences, the algorithm interprets each viewer's evolving interactions – what they watch, pause, skip, or rewatch – to predict and surface content that aligns with their shifting interests. This responsiveness mirrors the agility of a business that thrives on fluidity, rapidly recalibrating its communications to sustain engagement. By dynamically reshaping the customer experience at speed, Netflix demonstrates a core principle of dynamic coherence: a company's ability to learn, adapt, and respond in the moment rather than adhering to rigid programming or top-down planning.

Cohesion through Flow

Flow is a design concept from a fundamental law of physics (Professor Adrian Bejan calls it The Constructal Law (Bejan, 2012)). The law states that the configuration of systems evolve in such a way as to provide easier access to the currents that flow through it. Everything that moves is a flow system, including social organizations. They evolve to flow faster, smoother, and better. They are constantly morphing and changing in this direction. The smoother and faster flowing design emerges, without the imposition of power or control. The Constructal Law embraces all complex evolving systems, including those social organizations that are firms (Wong et al., 2023).

The phase change of the post-managerial era of capitalism is from managed hierarchical power structures to dynamically cohesive flow systems.

The flow system approach solves two major problems caused by the command-and-control model: (1) it erases the hierarchical power structure that has historically been utilized to pursue control; (2) it re-engages the individuals who are alienated and disengaged in the control system. These problems are solved along three dimensions:

Structure and Form: Traditionally, firm structures have been viewed as primarily static, providing strength and maintaining resilience against the buffetings of change and market turbulence. Once methods and processes are established, they bring structures into place for their consistent implementation. A structure might occasionally be adjusted in an event that's often called restructuring or re-organization, emphasizing just what a big undertaking is required to make that adjustment. In a flow state, dynamic structure becomes a tool for change and motion. Flow requires that we think differently about structure, and we may want to discard the use of the term entirely for business organizations.

Analogies from nature that provide alternatives to structure include the human circulatory system, designed for optimized blood flow which exhibits distinctive form and features, or the tensegrity concept from architecture and robotics that combines tension and compression to mimic bio-skeletal systems. The image of a cheetah sprinting across the landscape is sometimes invoked, with change of speed and change of direction and high responsiveness to external conditions and stimuli, while maintaining physical form. Or a flock of birds, cohesive because each individual follows the same simple ruleset, but without fixed structure.

Whatever the analogy, the point about flow systems for firms is a new and nonrestrictive thinking that replaces structure. Adaptability, flexibility, and resilience are emphasized above the control and predictability that have been the traditional concerns of management.

Knowledge flow: What flows in a flow state organization? The primary flow is knowledge – the new knowledge that results from interactions with external environments, markets and customers, and the feedback loops they generate, and the accumulated, shared knowledge that results from internal interactions and internal feedback loops. Knowledge-comes from action, and building proficiency through action is the fundamental cause of a firm's long-term performance (Madden, 2020). The free, accelerated, efficient flow of knowledge boosts this performance. Flow organizations are more adept at engineering flows of knowledge from customer and market interactions, and directing the flow internally as the raw material for improvement and innovation.

There are other flows as well. Value – the subjective experience of customers finding their expectations met to their satisfaction also flows from markets to the firm, and when it takes the form of exchange value, it directly triggers cash flow, which is the best financial measure of performance.

Engagement: We can also think of flow in its psychic form of individual experience, which contributes to the high engagement and commitment of colleagues and teams in a shared purpose that brings them meaning. When colleagues are free to align their own skills and interests with business tasks, and to utilize their own creativity in solving business problems, they become more absorbed in their work, feeling more fulfilment and achieving more innovation through intrinsic motivation. Flow can become an organization-wide phenomenon that raises firm performance.

Weaving a Constraint Regime through Flow

Management as control can be replaced by a principle of coherence that we can think of as the flow of a constraint regime. Every individual firm represents a context for self-organization into coherent dynamics.

The firm that elevates freedom over power, and replaces structure with flow in both its physics form (flow of knowledge) and its psychic form (flow of engagement) can think about its capabilities from a new perspective. It doesn't need to build departments and management hierarchies. It can identify the capabilities required to fulfill its purpose and cluster them for complementary dynamic implementation.

Figure 2 illustrates the elemental architecture of an interwoven constraint regime that shapes the purpose of the firm.

Needs Identification

The purpose of all economic activity is to address people's needs. People want to improve their circumstances, and are motivated to identify the best means to do so. At any point in time, they harbor multiple needs, perhaps ordered in a loose hierarchy (some are more important to them than others). Firms have emerged as one of the important ways to address people's needs – first by

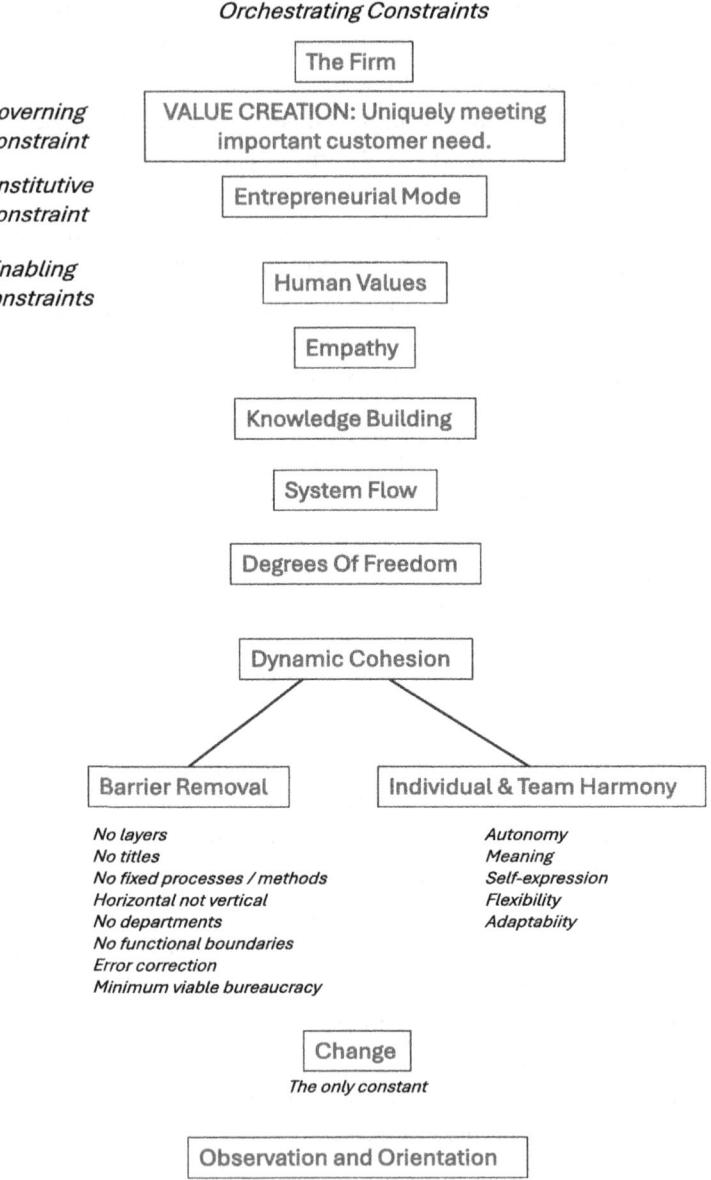

Figure 2 Constraint regime architecture.

identifying and understanding them, and then by designing commercial offerings as solutions, subject to customers' choices and evaluation.

This is a primary constraint: to be able to identify the needs or needs the firm will address. This capacity operates as a governing constraint: if the firm is to be significant, the need must be important and experienced by many people. It must be currently unmet, and the firm must be able to devise a way to meet it not only effectively but in a superior and differentiated manner. It's a tall order.

All firms must be defined this way by the needs that they meet. It's not easy, because needs are feelings that customers find hard to articulate. Needs must be deduced by firms. Deduction from incomplete knowledge can be dangerously inaccurate. It can also generate explosive growth when the need turns out to be more important than anticipated.

The Google search bar addressed a very important, probably universal need: the search for information. Its new technique of page ranking provided a superior solution, in an environment of internet expansion where the volume of accessible information was growing, increasing the satisfaction of searchers when they were able to find what they were looking for. Notice the key emotional variable here: satisfaction. It's a feeling, resulting from comparing experienced outcomes to anticipatory expectations. It's not necessarily rational and it is certainly not fixed. Today, we hear of dissatisfaction from Google searchers because their experience now involves clutter and sponsored links and advertising that some feel is disappointing compared to their expectations. The need for information is beginning to manifest itself in increasing usage of AI chatbot interfaces that provide a simultaneously richer and cleaner information-search experience than the original Google search bar. Needs are moving targets.

All firms must be defined by the need they address, and the associated feelings in the customer's mind. Emotion is the key to success. Not many firms think this way. The product-first mindset, even among our strongest technology companies, is a negative constraint that can result in a loss of focus on the emotions that matter.

Value Creation

The capability required to first identify and subsequently successfully meet important needs is value creation. This constraint of value creation is often misconceived because value is widely misunderstood. Firstly, it's customer value. Generating customer value is the first task. Concepts like shareholder value and stakeholder value are extractions that can only come into being as secondary effects after customer value is created. Value is the feeling of anticipated and then realized satisfaction in the mind of the customer. It's generated by firms that can stimulate that anticipation with a promise of a satisfaction experience and can support the realization with an outcome that matches or exceeds the anticipation and does so better – in the subjective evaluation of particular customers – than any alternative. Value creation is the power of the customer, not the power of management.

When well understood, value creation can be made into a discipline in the flow organization. Curt Carlson, a leader in the field of systematic innovation and former CEO of Stanford Research International (SRI) which was a world leader in applied innovation during his time there, calls for Continuous Value Creation as a standard for firms, just as mass production was in Ford's time or total quality was in Deming's time (Carlson, 2006). The discipline can be supported by processes to identify and develop deep knowledge of customers, deduce important unmet needs, design value propositions for customers to consider, and all the testing and development steps to bring the value proposition to the market as a new product or service. It's an enabling constraint.

The underpinning for the discipline and its processes is the understanding of subjective value. Customers decide what is valuable. They do the evaluating. Their process is qualitative – they personally attribute value to experiences. There's a predictive valuation (before the experience) and an assessment valuation (after the experience) (Packard, 2022). If the assessment valuation is positive, the future predictive valuation will be positive based on this new value knowledge. Value is a cycle, continuous and subject to adjustment. The role of what we call value creation is to facilitate the cyclical value process so that the customer experiences higher states of well-being. That's why Curt Carlson insists on continuous value creation as a constraint. It's hard, active, never-ending work.

Human Values

The positive psychology or psychic flow (Csikszentmihalyi, 1990) of the post-managerial paradigm is built on humanism and respect for human values. There is a value flow from customers to the firm, expressed in the empathic diagnosis of customer needs (Hastings, 2022) that ultimately translates into innovation and value realization. And there is a value flow between people in a networked organization, where each one can find purpose in meaning within the shared values of the firm. The authority hierarchy is replaced with the freedom and autonomy that open the way for unprecedented levels of engagement to propel economic achievement through value creation.

Empathy

The hard work of value creation conforms to the constraint of empathy. In the flow organization, empathy is the replacement for power, in two regards. First, empathy for customers drives innovation and value creativity. Empathy is a sympathetic understanding of the customer's emotional reasons for assigning value to one set of choices compared to another. Their assignment of value may or may not be rational, but it is not a monetary calculation so much as it is an act of imagination. Whether they know it or not, the act of choosing is an act of imagining a better future which hasn't arrived yet.

Management has no techniques for imagining the better future. It's not possible to imagine what the customer is imagining. But creative individuals can simulate that imagination. Just as a video game simulates reality, and a computer model simulates tomorrow's weather before it gets here, it is possible to simulate what another person might be imagining. How? A tool often used in science is the mental model. An observer or researcher can construct a model of how others think, how they make choices, and the value assessment tools they use. Having established the mental model customers are using, firms can design experiments that they imagine might fit that mental model, triggering positive evaluations, and the prospect of utility, pleasure, and satisfaction. The better the firm understands the customer's mental model, the greater the likelihood of success.

This process is human-to-human. It's not the analysis of big data sets. It's more intuitive than it is hard science. Some individuals are more empathic than others, but empathy is a business skill that can be learned, practiced, and nurtured in entrepreneurial mode. Importantly, it's not managerial, it's entrepreneurial. Those individuals who take the power and control approach to business will find it difficult to succeed.

The second application of empathy is in internal influence with colleagues. Empathy brings collaborative strength to teams, communities, and social networks, and underpins high-performing groups. Professor Dacher Keltner (Keltner, 2016) reports that empathy is the much superior alternative to the power of authority, position, or title. It brings a focus on others, and on nurturing their capabilities, contributions, and collaborative potential. Firms that are constructed pyramidically, with a hierarchy of authority, tend to lose this focus, and suffer an empathy deficit, according to Professor Keltner, whereby people at the lower levels of the hierarchy – those who are powerless – become disconnected from shared goals and concerns. Firms, where empathy networks are highly developed, are both more cohesive internally and better equipped to develop strong external relationships with customers and suppliers. Empathy has direct effects on business performance and is therefore a required element of a firm's constraint regime.

Knowledge Building and Scalable Learning

Empathy requires deep knowledge of customers and of the broader ecosystems in which they are embedded – in other words, of their lives and lived experience.

Knowledge-building – that is, active learning – proficiency is a fundamental driver of a firm's performance (Madden, 2020). Knowledge-building is a part of everyone's job, and improvement and innovation tend to advance spontaneously as shared knowledge-building experiences generate insights and expose faulty assumptions.

The best culture for knowledge-building is one of humility: acknowledging that there is much we don't know or understand, and that we will keep an open mind to new discoveries and revelations. All hypotheses must be tested in order to improve theory and eliminate faulty assumptions. Firms can establish an active learning environment with internal forums and exchanges (Curt Carlson, the former SRI CEO calls them "watering holes" (Carlson, 2006)) where hypotheses are challenged in a peer-review format. Externally, knowledge-building is a never-ending journey of traversing feedback loops to make new knowledge discoveries: design an experiment to which the customer can cogently and effectively respond in a way that will add to the firm's understanding and knowledge. The most valuable form of response is behavioral: did or did not buy, did or did not repeat purchase, did or did not recommend to others.

The digitally enabled firms of the twenty-first century, such as Handu (see p56), have a business model advantage in knowledge-building. They are digitally direct-connected to end-user customers via the internet, and continuously experimenting with new offers, new designs, new incentives, and new value propositions, all of which generate an immediate response of buying or not buying. Flows of data enter the Handu middle layer and back end, where they can be analyzed for patterns and novelty, and fed forward into further improvements and innovations to be evaluated via the next cycle of direct end-user interaction. This is fast-response, low cost, scalable learning (Fischer, Lago, & Lui, 2013) at high speed. The learning constraint has a high energy demand as well as high return on the energy expended.

Entrepreneurial Mode: Emergent Cohesion within the Constraint Regime

The interwoven constraint regime of needs identification, value creation based in human values, empathy, and scaled knowledge-building and learning enables the major shift from managerial mode to entrepreneurial mode. Firms that operate in entrepreneurial mode do so from a different set of principles and in a different way from those in managerial mode. They don't conform to any management handbook. Entrepreneurial mode is the post-managerial paradigm, exhibiting distinctively different characteristics.

Founder's Intent

All firms originate from founder's intent. This intent provides the birthing energy and imparts growth momentum. Vision and mission are wrapped in founder's intent. There's an emotional drive and commitment to succeed and the hardened realism of capital at risk, which guarantees that decisions will be rapid and precise in response to market data. The entrepreneurial ethic of serving others to improve their lives reaches its highest development in founders. There is pragmatic management of costs to provide service efficiently and profitably – no fluff. The colleagues and followers of the founder are steeped in the same vision and mission and totally united in their joint valuation creation efforts.

Even after founders have departed as a result of retirement or exit, firms in entrepreneurial mode are able to maintain founder's intent. It's a critical continuity to preserve and sustain the unique market relevance of the firm. The next generation of the firm's leaders and managers can recite the original mission with the same urgency and hunger as the original founders. There is no loss of veracity or authenticity.

Airbnb CEO Brian Chesky expands the concept of founder's intent into a system of management he calls founder mode (Graham, 2024). According to Chesky, an experienced and successful CEO, the conventional wisdom about how to run larger companies – which he calls manager mode – is mistaken. Founder mode carries the influence of founder's intent all the way to the details of implementation. In fact, Chesky advises that CEOs "live in the details" (Chesky, Gordon, 2025). Chesky added by way of advice to CEOs: stay small, stay flat, stay functional, have as few layers as possible, hire your own people, review all work, lean into a crisis, rethink everything. Founder mode – also called venture mode – is the opposite of management mode. CEOs should spend their time on design, not executive function, and Chesky provides a perspective on a completely different way of managing.

Value Flow

The foundation for all entrepreneurial firms is their concept of value. The key insight of value flow is that revenue follows as a consequence of value creation, and the firm can then establish a cost structure to deliver customer value at a profit, which is necessary in order to sustain the business. There is no "cost-cutting." Cost is a strategic choice to support value creation.

The value mindset – to create customer value as a first priority with the confidence that revenue and profits will follow – is foundational for the entrepreneurial mode. It is not captured in strategy or planning or business administration. It is captured in empathy.

In entrepreneurial mode, firms internalize the mindset that customers draw value from the firm to themselves. Entrepreneurs humbly submit to the decisions of the consumer.

The Entrepreneurial Ethic

The value mindset and the empathic approach to customers combine to produce a distinct entrepreneurial ethic. The reason for being in business in the first place is to make customers feel better about their own circumstances. Businesses can do this if they have a good understanding why customers will feel better and empathizing with their motivation. Those two characteristics – understanding and empathizing – are the foundations of the business ethic. There is no room for exploitation or insincerity or over-promising or under-delivery. The service ethic is the entrepreneurial business driver. The service is always an offering, or what is sometimes called a value proposition. The decision to accept it is always with the customer, and the evaluation of the experience after the offer is accepted is also entirely in the customer's domain. The entrepreneurial mode is characterized by humility. It's a process of learning from customers and markets rather than one of setting strategy and making plans.

The entrepreneurial ethic can change attitudes to business at multiple levels. The teams within the firm can take inspiration and meaning from the work of improving customers' lives. Business partners can be motivated by participating in the customer value pie and earning their piece. And outside observers, especially young people who sometimes question the ethics of business and corporations, can be persuaded to rethink their negativity. Service to others as the purpose of business activity is an elevating idea.

Differentiation through Fitting In

In the old management paradigm, differentiation is viewed as a strategic weapon for advantage in beating competition. But with the service ethic as their standard, entrepreneurially minded businesses seek to fit in rather than stand out, by finding the part of the ecosystem where they can create superior value in customers' eyes. This differentiation is based on two complementary components of entrepreneurship. The first is knowing and understanding a specific group of customers really well, and better than any other firm. Knowledge and understanding go deeper than demographics and survey research, or purchase records and response to email campaigns and digital marketing metrics. Entrepreneurial mode relies on understanding customers' lives. The relationship with customers is a whole-life relationship. Life is a system with multiple interconnecting channels and strands of behaviors and interactions and cross-dependencies. This is as true of the life of a household as it is of the life of an office or the life of a factory. Entrepreneur mode maps out the complete system.

The second component is to creatively contribute something new to make the system work even better without disrupting it. Improving customers' lives includes making their life systems work better. This is systems thinking at a highly refined level – thinking of the future system and how it will evolve. Entrepreneurial mode embraces an evolving purpose of continuously enhancing already complex systems. When a customer can discern that a particular firm has the improvement of their system in mind as its purpose, and has the unmatched idiosyncratic know-how and understanding to bring about that purpose, then high differentiation results.

Qualitative, Not Quantitative

Business thinking and business education are dominated by quantification. To "make the numbers" is the highest accolade for management. Everything must be measured, and what gets measured gets done. Both financialization and digitization have strongly influenced this mindset. Financialization imposes quantitative targets from third-party analysts: quarterly earnings, returns on capital, operating ratios, subscriber growth targets, profit margins, free cash flow targets, and many, many more. These metrics are increasingly short-sighted, as metric horizons shrink from quarterly to monthly to weekly to daily.

The obsession with quantification is related to the increasing dominance of left-brain thinking in society highlighted by Dr. Iain McGilchrist (McGilchrist, The Matter With Things: Our brains, Our Delusions, and the Unmaking of the World, 2021). It is the analytical, reductionist, and detail-focused preferences of the brain's left-hemisphere that results in the focus on utility and measurement of explicit phenomena, suppressing intuitive thought and underweighting qualitative factors like trust, intuition, and narrative.

Digitization has made the obsession with numbers even more intense, since many more business activities and results are measurable: page views, click-throughs, conversion ratios, lifetime customer value, cost of customer acquisition, advertising performance by channel, platform and individual website, by hour, minute, and second. Digital marketing has been especially destructive of the emotional connection between companies, their brands, and their consumers. How much love is the customer feeling? It's not deemed relevant by today's marketers since they can place a numerical value on the number of clicks.

In entrepreneurial mode, the fixation with numbers, while never completely relinquished, is tempered by a deeper understanding of the role of qualitative measures such as customer insights, emotional engagement, levels of empathy, personal values, social ties, perceptions, preferences, and expectations. Qualities that can't be measured are the ones that are most important to building strong customer relationships, engaging and enthusing employees, and forging strong business partnerships. Entrepreneurial businesses are at their best when they demonstrate a shared confidence in the application of qualitative measures in navigating toward the generation of subjective value.

Discovering cohesion includes rebalancing qualitative insights and the quantitative resources of data and metrics.

Networks, Not Hierarchies

Perhaps the greatest impediment for firms to creatively and adaptively navigate markets is the hierarchical structure of authority in traditional management models. Every idea and action must be cleared by the level above. The result is slowness and delay, loss of customer and market insights, and dampened enthusiasm for initiative-taking.

Dynamic cohesion is an outcome of networks, not hierarchies. Networks can put every role on the same level, to a great extent, and can maximize the information flow from the customer and the market, and between nodes. Entrepreneurial mode networks span the firm horizontally without divisional or departmental or functional demarcations, and vertically insofar as there are any levels at all. The network is the organizational structure of entrepreneurial firms, without boxes on org charts, differentiated titles, or power authority. Flow of knowledge and value is the driver of decision-making rather than the power or authority of position.

Action over Strategy

Strategy has long been one of the most prized elements of intellectual property in management science, and a business school with a reputation for excellence in the field of strategy gathers disproportionate prestige. But strategy is not so important in entrepreneurial mode, for the simple reason that strategy is an attempt to predict and control, or at least influence the future. The entrepreneurial mindset embraces the truth that the future is unpredictable, the result of billions and trillions of micro-interactions between individuals, firms, markets, and institutions that can't be monitored, let alone controlled.

The entrepreneurial mode prioritizes action over strategy. Entrepreneurship is a process of exploration and discovery. Exploration can be guided by purpose – that is, for these specific customers, to enhance this specific benefit area – but is primarily experimental. Try this, try that. Tech companies often use the term A/B test, where A and B are alternative actions to achieve the benefit result, and their respective performances are experimentally compared so that a decision can be made regarding which action to take. There is no preference or judgment in favor of one versus the other. Strategy is replaced by A/B testing, creating new knowledge rather than trying to centralize what is already known.

The feedback loop is integral to the action paradigm. Action is in the market, with the customer's approval and selection in mind. The feedback loop is the customer's communication of their evaluation of an experience. It can be transmitted through repeat purchase and loyalty, or through choosing a competitive offering next time around. It can be comments or ratings or word of mouth. It can come in the form of a strengthening or weakening perception or brand image, or increased or decreased attention to advertising. The action-minded entrepreneurial firm is more comfortable with action data, actual behaviors regarding purchase and usage or even clicks, rather than opinions expressed in surveys. The empathic entrepreneurial mind can deduce attitudes from behavior; casually expressed opinions are less reliable.

Bureaucracy Busting

Bureaucracy is the enemy of entrepreneurial value creation. Bureaucracy exists in business firms for two reasons. First to standardize practices and processes; and second, to enable executive and managerial control over the actions of subordinate roles in the firm. Entrepreneurial mode rejects both reasons.

Standardization, while potentially a pathway to efficiency, represses creativity and innovation. Efficiency is a benefit to the firm in the form of greater output for the same or less input, but not necessarily for the customer. The entrepreneurial employee who is closest to the customer may spot some non-standard opportunity to adjust a service for better fit with the customer system, yet be prevented from implementing it as a violation of a bureaucratic standard. Entrepreneurial mode prefers adaptiveness and responsiveness, without first seeking permission.

The bureaucracy of control is induced by the existence of hierarchical layers. Top executives and "chiefs" decide on policies, and communicate them to senior, intermediate, and junior managers, so that they eventually reach the lower levels or front lines as instructions to follow. This requires not only written communications in the form of handbooks and policy manuals but also digital administration in the form of templates and data fields to fill out. And, most of all, it requires meetings. Many executive and managerial days are spent in back-to-back meetings. Meetings are the primary weapon of the bureaucratic forces. Meetings take place to selectively filter, package, and repackage information so that its transmission can be coordinated across departments and divisions and functions, and vertically between levels.

Entrepreneurial mode obviates the need for bureaucracy and its meetings by eliminating layers and organizing functions as horizontal fields rather than divisionalized silos. Layers can be replaced by self-managing teams pursuing purpose-directed goals with coordinated team actions. Information is processed at the team level, and meetings are fewer in number and kept short (such as the daily "standup" meeting of agile software teams, so named because sitting down would be characteristic of an unnecessarily long meeting).

Previously siloed functions can be reframed as shared tasks with a singular purpose, as captured, for example, in the expression "everyone does marketing." This means that the goal of marketing, customer satisfaction, is one that everyone in the firm shares and for which they accept responsibility, and the function of marketing is the integration of all those individual marketing acts that take place all over the company into a unified relationship that can be encapsulated as a trusting relationship or, more simply, a brand. Meetings don't accomplish this integration; aligned actions do.

Entrepreneurial mode avoids bureaucracy and meetings whenever possible. Bureaucracy is defined as action and associated allocated time where the primary purpose is not value creation for the customer but internal coordination. Actions with a low customer value score are abandoned or reduced to a minimum.

Individualism and Autonomy

The entrepreneurial tradition is born of individual freedom. Popular literature often portrays "the entrepreneur" as the brave and creative loner, fighting for market acceptance of his or her brilliantly innovative but not-yet-fully-appreciated new product. There is a business role for individual creativity of course, but it is more important for the growth and progress of the economy that whole team and business units and firms and corporations are entrepreneurial.

The entrepreneurial mode is the intentional pursuit of new economic value. This definition pulls together multiple interdependent concepts. Intentionality is the energizing long-term disposition to create value. There may be twists and turns along the way, surges of growth and periods of setbacks, learning through error correction and negative feedback, but through it all, the intention remains firm. Pursuit confirms that value creation is a process, both dynamic and time consuming, and requiring the acceptance of uncertainty, because a pursuit is not guaranteed to capture the prize. Entrepreneurship proceeds in spite of uncertainty in the confidence that adaptive creativity will eventually lead to a good outcome. New economic value refers to innovation and the improvement in customer lives through the innovation of new goods and services that customers deem useful and valuable. All of these are inherent in entrepreneurial mode, and the mode can be adopted at any organizational level.

Yet still, the ultimate source of entrepreneurial energy is the free minded and creatively resourceful individual. Entrepreneurial mode is defined by action, and all actions are ultimately individual actions. Whether working in teams or units, or advancing coordinated projects, or contributing to group goals by working on shared tasks, the autonomy and freedom of the individual is always critical. Individuals are the source of ideas, and individuals in collaboration improve total productivity.

Generative Business Models

A typical result from these entrepreneurial mode principles is a systematic value creation business model designed to produce and sustain continuous innovation, growth, or value over time, often by leveraging the network effects and feedback loops inherent in the digital economy. These models are discovered more than designed.

There are a few key aspects of generative business models that entrepreneurial mode highlights:

User-driven Value Creation: Since entrepreneurial mode focuses tightly on the end user, and specifically on understanding their most urgent needs and wants, entrepreneurs structure business models in such a way that users, customers, or participants contribute to generating new value. They do this by interacting with the business platform, especially to get things done. This way, users purposefully share data with the business, from which entrepreneurial mode deduction draws insights and recognizes patterns. Entrepreneurial mode emphasizes marketplaces and ecosystems where user participation drives further engagement and accelerates and multiplies value creation.

Network Effects: Entrepreneurial mode is especially attuned to the power of networks since creative entrepreneurs seek to combine and recombine assets and resources that they don't necessarily own or command. As they engage more users with their expanding service network, its value increases, leading to exponential growth. Generative models are often built to scale rapidly as network effects amplify their impact, as seen in platforms like Airbnb or Uber, both started by under-resourced entrepreneurs aiming to assemble a network of similarly under-resourced collaborators to create value together.

AI and Automation: Entrepreneurial mode eagerly seeks ways to increase capacity without adding fixed assets, and AI and automation are a perfect fit. More and more AI tools are emerging for entrepreneurs to use and explore, resulting in new outputs, services, or innovations with minimal additional human input.

Open-ended Innovation: Entrepreneurs love models that are not limited to a single product or service offering but are designed to enable ongoing innovation. They prefer unbounded opportunity spaces with the chance to explore without necessarily having a fixed destination in mind. They are not afraid of experimentation, comfortable in the knowledge that markets will select those experiments that work for them and meet their needs, sending the feedback to the entrepreneur about where to expand their efforts and which dead-end paths to abandon.

Cohesion Can't Come from Management

The cohesion of the needs-driven, value creating, empathic, knowledge building entrepreneurial mode firm is not a structure but a flow. Cohesively flowing organizations evolve and emerge as vibrant, responsive environments where knowledge flows freely and without obstruction, enabling teams to innovate, make rapid decisions, adapt quickly to change, and in some cases anticipate it.

Dr. Adrian Bejan observes (Bejan, Adrian, Design In Nature: How The Constructal Law Governs Evolution In Biology, Physics, Technology And Social Organization, 2012, p9) that, if the system is free, it demonstrates a natural tendency to reconfigure for easier flow: systems "endow themselves" with design or, in other words, self-organize. Flow designs get measurably better, moving more easily and farther.

In business, flow organizations self-organize to optimize the flows most relevant to business success. We can define these primary flows as knowledge and interaction capital.

Flow of knowledge – both tacit and explicit – is at the heart of the flow organization. This flow is essential for decision-making, innovation, value creation, and customer satisfaction. The explosion of knowledge in the twenty-first century gives rise to a new system logic: the need to transform knowledge into a fundamental element of production, whether physical (better design of products and services) or intellectual (better knowledge realization in brands, patents, processes, etc.) (Nascimento, 2021). Knowledge flow and transformation becomes a driver of competitive performance.

Knowledge flow is the foundation of innovation, problem-solving, and organizational adaptability, with firms increasingly recognizing the importance of their absorptive capacity (the ability of a firm to identify, assimilate and use external knowledge) and the role of emerging technologies in supporting knowledge dissemination (Oo & Rakthin, 2022).

The focus is on removing structural barriers that impede the flow of knowledge. For organizations to stay cohesive, they must evolve to ensure that knowledge processing mechanisms are optimized to handle large-scale and real-time data, enabling teams to make faster, more informed decisions. This aligns with constructal theory, which posits that systems must continuously evolve to enhance the flow of currents, whether they be knowledge or energy, for long-term sustainability (Bejan, 2008) (Freire, 2018)

Bartley J. Madden describes a holistic knowledge flow and value creation system that establishes a knowledge-building culture to support every knowledge application from strategy to organization to functional performance in current businesses and innovation in existing and new ones, and to context-specific measurement (Madden, 2024). In other words, knowledge flow can drive all aspects of business.

Flow of ideas: The cohesive organization places its emphasis on fresh perspectives, and openly invites, celebrates and develops new ideas. In people, it values potential over experience and historical achievement. There is no climbing the corporate ladder; politics is replaced with creative ideation. Collaborative engagement results in the cross-pollination of ideas into compounded growth initiatives. Intellectual energy drives the system.

Experimental flow: One of the biggest drawbacks of the old management paradigm in the new business era is its overdeveloped defense of the status quo and consequent difficulties with adaptive change. The solution is a flow of experimentation. New experiments can be spun up quickly because there are no barriers put in the way if experimenters. Rapid feedback cycles keep the flow moving, and easy reallocation of resources enables the adjustment to feedback. Learning is prized and not seen as failure, and many parallel exploration paths can be pursued simultaneously.

Flow of interaction capital: In the twenty-first century, business success will be increasingly determined not by the traditional focus areas of management, but by the quality and quantity and speed of interactions that occur within an organization and between the organization and its environment. Interaction capital includes all the flows of value that arise from these interactions, including:

- **Financial flows:** Cash flow is the primary indicator of value creation, since it is generated directly from interactions with customers, including exchange transactions, contracts, subscriptions, retainers, and fees, which all represent interaction capital. Similarly, investment flows originate in interactions with investors, funds, banks, and private equity. Internally, financial flows include allocation of resources and investments in internal and external innovation projects, where interaction capital includes value propositions, pitches and presentations, and collaborative workshops.

- **Reputation and brand strength:** The trust and loyalty built through consistent and meaningful interactions with customers, end users, partners, and colleagues are exhibited in intangibles such as brand perception and a company's reputation. These are qualitative and subjective attributes, but trackable in various ways (surveys and customer research) which will indicate progress or decline.
- **Social network strength:** The networks of trust, recognition, and collaboration within teams and across the organization become stronger and stronger as interaction capital is built. Innovative ideas flow more freely, internal engagement and morale are higher, customers and partners are more closely bonded and more loyal, everyone feels free to contribute, and collective intelligence is enhanced.

The flow of interaction capital can become both a core competitive advantage for the sustainability of an agile, innovative, and resilient firm, and a source of internal strength and cohesion. In a firm that's rich in interaction capital, there emerges a culture of open communication and collaboration, idea sharing, feedback, and fully aligned cross-functional cocreation. Individuals can experience a psychic flow state (Csikszentmihalyi, 1990) of immersion in stimulating shared tasks where a sense of personal mastery can be enhanced by collective expertise. With a constant flow of information, whether it's customer data, market insights, or internal innovation ideas, individuals refine their skills as they work with ever-evolving knowledge. The availability of knowledge combined with the freedom to experiment, iterate, and improve nurtures a fertile environment for individuals to engage ever more deeply in their tasks, thereby entering flow.

High levels of interaction capital also mean that individuals and teams are constantly receiving recognition and feedback, helping them to grow in their roles. Recognition and promotion are part of the broader interaction capital that an individual can accrue in a firm – interacting with others who have more experience to share, and with external suppliers and stakeholders who validate their work. A continuous cycle of challenge, feedback, and recognition supports people in stretching their own abilities, leading to personal flow and professional growth. There's a feeling of fulfilment in current tasks and a potential pathway for advancement to greater degrees of mastery in the future.

Flow states can become norms within a firm's culture. Teams regularly enter collective flow during collaborative problem-solving sessions, creative workshops, and intensive project sprints. Collective engagement boosts overall performance and drives the organization forward, as individuals and teams push the boundaries of what's possible through interactions that are fluid, free, and rich. There's a culture of continuous improvement where personal goals are fully aligned with organizational success.

Is There Any Role for Managers?

Traditional management uses power and control in an attempt to constrain uncertainty and limit outcomes to a narrow range of preferred probabilities. Traditional management has operated in a way to limit the freedom of interaction and, often, to block the emergence of rich and free-flowing states.

One choice open to firms is no management – a complete abandonment of traditional ways. This is the philosophy of self-management at The Morning Star Company and so-called liberated firms like Favi. They are liberating themselves from management. When Morning Star founder Christopher Rufo established the two principles of no coercion and voluntary keeping of commitments, he eradicated any role for management, which coerces with top-down decision-making and specifies behavioral norms. The innovation of no layers, no titles, no fixed processes or methods, no departments, no functional boundaries and horizontal rather than vertical form is nonmanagement.

Complex adaptive systems theory would support the nonmanagement approach. Emergence of new patterns results from unpredictable nonlinear system behavior. It can't be managed.

If we think at the level of the ecosystem, this completely hands-off approach leads to the best outcomes. In the ecosystem of automobile transportation, for example, the emergent outcome over 130 years has brought us the experience of 200 mph supercars, ultra-efficient small cars, long-lasting everyday sedans, electric vehicles, and multiuse pickup trucks. During that time, many individual manufacturing firms have gone out of business, which was part of the system evolving freely over time so that trapped assets could be put to greater use.

If we think at the level of the subsystem, such as the firm, and if waiting for emergence in a completely hands-off mode is not the favored choice, what is to be done in the absence of management? The answer lies in freeing and facilitating.

Freeing and Facilitating

There is a role at the firm level for entrepreneurial action that accelerates flow and facilitates value creation.

Identify and Monitor the Ecosystem

A firm is a contributor to a bigger ecosystem, and, reciprocally, the ecosystem is the location for both unmet customer needs and new technological developments. A firm in free-flowing cohesion mode will identify the relevant ecosystem precisely and monitor the trends and changes that open up new opportunities in the form of a potential future.

Identification of the ecosystem is facilitated by empathy, because the ecosystem must be viewed from the customer's point of view. To contribute to the automobile transportation ecosystem, a firm views it through the customer's eyes. The relevant ecosystem is family life. A family may draw from this ecosystem for educational purposes (driving the kids to school), for nutrition (driving to the grocery store), for earning a living (driving to work or to a customer's location), and for recreation (driving to the beach). Each of these subjectively valued purposes is facilitated by different attributes: space, comfort, reliability, carrying capacity, safety. In-use characteristics are also ecosystem related: ease of accessing fuel, efficient use of fuel, maintenance costs, onboard technology for everything from entertainment to navigation software to performance monitoring, and outboard technology like Apple Car Play and external cameras and tires. The user's ecosystem includes many interconnecting relationships that may be hard to uncover and understand. Assembling a guidebook to the ecosystem through knowledge creation and knowledge flow facilitates the creation of future value by illuminating new areas to fit in and contribute.

Within the ecosystem, many players are pursuing their own opportunities, and their activities can modify the ecosystem. Expect continuous change and monitor it.

Configuring the Subsystem to Interact

Ecosystems accept and welcome subsystems that are configured to fit in and contribute new or additional value. The automobile ecosystem embraced digital navigation tools like Google Maps because users were already engaged in navigation, and GPS systems made navigation easier, especially when fully integrated into the driving cockpit and the driving experience. Android Auto is Google's way of integrating the entire phone interface with the automobile experience, an example of hyper-personalization via fitting the subsystem into the larger ecosystem to facilitate new value.

As a B2B service, Android Auto also must fit in to the business system of supplier relationships and provide sales and business development interfaces where the knowledge flow includes an intimate understanding of the automobile manufacturers' needs.

In general, the firm is a value subsystem that can grow and succeed when it is optimally configured to contribute to a larger ecosystem. The process of configuration to fit in is generally thought of as design – the shape and structure and look and feel and experience of good fit.

Identifying Flows

As has been emphasized, the primary value-creation flow is knowledge. There is a wide range of knowledge flow and a high volume. The most useful knowledge for value creation is the knowledge that comes from the customer, whether it is quantitative behavioral data or qualitative data about preferences and opinions and their subjective evaluation of experiences. Business model designers can increase the flow of customer is via direct connection. In this case, flow *is* a business model. Businesses like Handu and the amazon.com online retail site have established just such a direct connection, so that knowledge flow (especially buying or not buying, but also reviews, preferred methods of payment, choice of delivery options, general trends and pattern changes in buyer preferences and behaviors over time) is rapidly channeled through networks at high volume to analysts (whether machine learning or artificial intelligence or human) who can transform it into new value propositions that flow back to customers and partners.

Other knowledge flows include knowledge of emerging new technologies, knowledge about the know-how and skills of the employee base (and enhancing that know-how through knowledge sharing such as training), and institutional knowledge that might range from regulations to the best schools for recruiting graduates.

Degrees of Freedom

Once the system and its flows are defined, the freeing and facilitating process begins with adding one degree of freedom at a time. Degrees of freedom are features that can be changed freely. The freeing process is to study how the changes to one feature facilitate an increase in the flows that are identified as most important in the system. Then the process frees a second feature and studies the effects, and then a third and so on. Freeing and facilitating is a dynamic approach that may never end. Those individuals who were formerly managers can take on new roles with this function, exploring different configurations before the optimum level of degrees of freedom is established.

Harmony through Alignment and Engagement

The degrees of freedom in the system require internal alignment, and management can be replaced by the internal development of mental models to replace direction and control with harmonization. The goal is an unburdened harmony both of the firm interacting with its external environment (markets, customers, suppliers) and harmony within the firm between producer teams.

Teams harmonized with a shared entrepreneurial intent develop a self-organized capacity to act as a network of people, things and narrative (shared meaning). They are characterized by fluidity of interaction and exchange. Individuals on a team are interdependent, and multiple teams can be interdependent with each other in the team of teams. Interdependency can cross boundaries (e.g., the marketing team might embrace both finance and operations) and between levels (e.g., combining planning and execution) because it is the quality of interactions that matter, not the structural arrangement of resources.

Individual Flow

In addition to the system flow achieved as result of removing barriers within the firm's business activities, adding degrees of freedom can be the catalyst for individual flow – Mihalyi Csikszentmihalyi's concept of a state of deep focus and immersion in an activity, where individuals experience a high degree of satisfaction, creativity, and productivity. Applied in business, flow can amplify autonomy, meaning, and commitment by encouraging employees to freely engage in challenging, yet achievable, tasks that align with their skills and interests. When teams experience flow, they are fully absorbed in their work, leading to heightened innovation and a stronger connection to business goals. It fosters intrinsic motivation, making work more fulfilling and purpose-driven. Csikszentmihalyi himself made the link between flow and "good business" (Csikszentmihalyi, 2003). Former managers can become flow catalysts.

10 Conclusion

The purpose of business and its firms is value creation – the facilitation of feelings of satisfaction and the pleasure of better circumstances. Management gets in the way.

That sounds like a harsh judgment, but it's an objective assessment of a well-intended human activity that developed in a direction that turned out to be opposed to the evolution of markets, favoring control rather than freedom. Management has proved to be a category error. Specifically, it is an error of agency, the idea of acting to exert control. In management, some must manage and others must be managed.

Knowledge is managed. Creativity is managed. Good outcomes are deemed to be caused by good management. Henry Fayol's five management functions of planning, organizing, leading, coordinating and controlling all stem from the overarching category error.

Management was born of the fear of not being able to control. The staff of the Prussian army feared losing control of the battlefield. George Whistler feared a rash of railroad accidents, and Frederick W. Taylor feared unrealized productivity. Fayol and a procession of followers took this lead. The antidote to fear was control, and control required the power of authority.

The dead end has been reached because we now understand that control is a chimera and authority can not produce the outcomes we want. The new knowledge that comes from complex adaptive systems theory to illuminate emergence, the new physics of flow systems, the new positive psychology of mental flow, and the new economics of entrepreneurship all combine in a new synthesis of spontaneous order.

We have yet to discover how best to apply the new synthesis in the post-managerial era, but we can be confident about leaving management behind. Whether the new order is self-management or Rendanheyi or digitally enabled autonomy is not yet clear, but we have set sail for new shores, under the banner of a new set of constraints which result in a firm with different characteristics than the structure, strategy, scale, and scope of the traditional paradigm.

The Emergent Characteristics of the Post-Managerial Paradigm

1 Ecosystemic Orientation

Organizations view themselves as nodes within dynamic ecosystems, cocreating value with customers, partners, communities, and even competitors. Rather than competing for market share in fixed industries, they foster interdependent networks that amplify collective impact and resilience. Purpose changes from dominating a market to enabling a thriving ecosystem, as Tesla does in electric vehicles and power systems.

2 Emergent Strategy and Sensemaking

Strategic planning is replaced by iterative learning through experimentation, feedback, and collective sensemaking. Organizations navigate uncertainty by testing hypotheses, learning from outcomes, and adapting in real time, guided by a shared purpose rather than fixed plans. Rigid, top-down planning is an anomaly, replaced by the complex systems theory's full embrace of complexity and uncertainty.

3 Distributed Agency and Fluid Roles

Authority and responsibility are distributed across self-organizing teams, with roles defined by context, skills, and needs rather than fixed titles or hierarchies. Employees shift fluidly between tasks, projects, and teams, enabled by trust and transparent information flows. This characteristic dismantles the old paradigm's centralized hierarchy and static roles, addressing anomalies like decision bottlenecks and suppressed innovation. It requires cultural shifts toward trust and accountability.

4 Value Cocreation with Customers

Customers are active participants in the value creation process, contributing ideas, feedback, and even content to shape products and services. Organizations design for cocreation, using platforms, communities, and real-time data to align offerings with evolving needs. This shifts the mechanistic production model to a participatory, outside-in approach, where value is relational, not transactional.

5 Purpose-Driven Culture and Pluralistic Voices

The shared purpose that characterizes the organization transcends profit, inspiring employees and stakeholders to align around greater shared impact. Diverse perspectives and constructive dissent are encouraged to fuel creativity and challenge assumptions, countering the old paradigm's suppression of dissent and short-term financial focus.

6 Adaptive Governance and Dismantling of Structures

Governance is lightweight, adaptive, and participative, using simple emergent protocols, aided by autonomous digital tools to coordinate action without rigid hierarchies or silos. Structures dissolve away as the organization evolves organically in response to needs and context.

7 Continuous Learning and Knowledge Flows

Organizations persist by prioritizing continuous learning, with knowledge shared freely across boundaries via communities of practice, wikis, or AI-driven insights. Employees are encouraged to experiment, reflect, and upskill, viewing failure as a learning opportunity. This runs counter to the old paradigm's reactive monitoring and coercive management, addressing anomalies like outdated metrics and demotivated workers. The focus is on dynamic, evolving states.

8 Long-Term Resilience and Regenerative Impact

Organizations prioritize long-term resilience over short-term gains, designing operations to regenerate resources, communities, and ecosystems. Metrics balance financial, social, and environmental outcomes, aligning with stakeholder expectations. Cohesion brings reality to the integration of exploration and exploitation, replacing old concepts of ambidextrousness (i.e., balancing both priorities) with the new recognition of dynamic flow that involves both without difference or distinction.

These characteristics taken together reflect a shift from a mechanistic, linear worldview to one of organic, flowing, relational cohesion. Thomas Kuhn argued the need for a new worldview as a pre-requisite for the emergence of a new paradigm.

This post-managerial paradigm provides the new worldview: business organizations as complex living value-creation systems, not machines.

References

Alexander, C. (1980). *The Nature of Order*. Berkeley, CA: The Center for Environmental Structure.

Alexander, C. (2020). *The Nature of Order, Book 2*. Berkeley, CA: The Center for Environmental Structure.

Arendt, H. (1958). *The Human Condition*. Chicago: University of Chicago Press.

Argyris, C. (1992). *On Organizational Learning*. Blackwell Publishers.

Arora, K. (2023). *The Gaming Industry: A Behemoth with Unprecedented Global Reach. Forbes.com*, November 17.

Axelrod, R., & Cohen, M. D. (2000). *Harnessing complexity: Organizational implications of a scientific frontier*. New York, NY: The Free Press.

Beatty, J. (1998). *The World According to Peter Drucker*. New York: The Free Press.

Bejan, A. (2008). *Design with Constructal Theory*. Wiley Interdisciplinary Reviews: Computational Molecular Science.

Bejan, A. (2012). *Design in Nature*. New York: Doubleday.

Bejan, A. (2020). *Freedom and Evolution: Hierarchy in Nature, Society and Science*. Cham: Springer.

Bennis, W. (2003). Thoughts on "The Essentials of Leadership." In ed. P. Graham, *Prophet of Management: A Celebration* (pp. 177–181). Washington, DC: Beard Books.

Béliczky, M. (2025, January 14). Adapting for success: The organizational shift every 21st century business needs. *LinkedIn*. https://www.linkedin.com/pulse/adapting-success-organizational-shift-every-21st-century-b%25C3%25A9liczky-i4phe/?trackingId=PKtbXOVZTeq%2BdyXLa18x2Q%3D%3D.

Boettke, P. J., Caceres, W. Z., & Martin, A. G. (2013). Error is obvious, coordination is the puzzle. In R. Frantz & R. Leeson (Eds.), *Hayek and behavioral economics* (pp. 90–110). London, England: Palgrave Macmillan. https://doi.org/10.1057/9781137278159_5.

Buchanan, J. M. (1979). *What should economists do?* Indianapolis, IN: Liberty Fund.

Bylund, P. L., & Packard, M. D. (2022). Back to the future: Can counterhistory accelerate theoretical advancement in management? *Journal of Management Inquiry, 31*(2), 139–146. https://doi.org/10.1177/10564926211007086.

Carlson, C. R. (2006). *Innovation: The Five Disciplines for Creating What Customers Want*. New York: Crown Publishing Group.

Cilliers, P. (1998). *Complexity and postmodernism: Understanding complex systems*. London, England: Routledge.

Collier, J. (2004). Self-organization, individuation and identity. *Revue Internationale de Philosophie*, *58*(2), 151–172.

Christensen, Clayton M. (1997). The innovator's dilemma: when new technologies cause great firms to fail. Harvard Business Review Press.

Csikszentmihalyi, M. (1990). *Flow: The Psychology of Optimal Experience*. New York: Harper and Row.

Csikszentmihalyi, M. (2003). *Good Business: Leadership, Flow and the Making of Meaning*. New York: Penguin Group.

Davis, T., & Higgins, J. (2013). A Blockbuster failure: How an outdated business model destroyed a giant. *Chapter 11 Bankruptcy Case Studies*, *11*. Retrieved from https://ir.law.utk.edu/utk_studlawbankruptcy/11.

Deming, W. E. (1982). *Out of the Crisis*. Boston, MA: MIT.

Drucker, P. (1959). *The Landmarks of Tomorrow*. New York: Harper and Row.

Drucker, P. (2006). *The Effective Executive*. New York: Harper Business.

Fayol, H. (1917). *Administration industriel et generale*. Paris: H. Dunod et E. Pinat.

Fernandez-Araoz, C. (2020). Jack Welch's Approach to Leadership. *Harvard Business Review*, March 3.

Fischer, B., Lago, U., & Lui, F. (2013). *Reinventing Giants: How Chinese Global Competitor Haier Has Changed the Way Big Companies Transform*. San Francisco: Jossey-Bass.

Freire, L. (2018). Constructal Law of Institutions within Social Organizations. *Open Journal of Applied Sciences*, 8 (3), 103–125.

Fruin, W. M. (1992). *The Japanese Enterprise System*. New York: Oxford University Press.

Getz, I. (2009). Liberating Leadership: How the Initiative-Freeing Radical Organizational Form Has Been Successfully Adopted. *California Management Review*, 51, 32–58.

Gilbert, P., Raulet-Croset, N., & Teglborg, A.-C. (2021). FAVI: A Managerial Innovation Built on Humanist Values. In ed. E. von Kimakowitz, *Humanistic Management in Practice* (pp. 171–185). Heidelberg: Springer Nature.

Gilbert, P., Teglborg, A.-C., & Raulet-Croset, N. (2018). *The Liberated Firm, a Radical Innovation or a Mere Avatar of Participatory Management*? Paris: Gerer Et Comprendre.

Goleman, D. (1995). *Emotional Intelligence*. Bantam Books.

Gordon, D. (2025, May 14). He revolutionized travel. Can Airbnb's founder redesign your entire life? *The Wall Street Journal Magazine*. https://www.wsj.com/articles/airbnb-ceo-brian-chesky-redesigning-travel-and-life-3e0b9e0b.

Graeber, D. (2015). *The Utopia of Rules*. London: Melville House.

Graham, P. (2024, September). Founder mode. *Paul Graham*. http://www.paulgraham.com/foundermode.html.

Gray, B., & Sarnak, D. O. (2015). *Home Care by Self-Governing Teams: The Netherlands' Buurtzorg Model*. New York: Commonwealth Fund.

Greeven, M. J., Xin, K., & Yip, G. S. (2023). How Chinese Companies Are Reinventing Management. *Harvard Business Review*, March–April.

Guerra, C., Capitelli, M., & Longo, S. (2012). The role of paradigms in science: A historical perspective. In L. L'Abate (Ed.), *Paradigms in Theory Construction* (pp. 19–30). New York, NY: Springer. https://doi.org/10.1007/978-1-4614-0914-4_2.

Hacking, I. (2012). Introductory Essay. In T. S. Kuhn, *The Structure of Scientific Revolutions* (50th Anniversary ed., pp. vii–xxxvii). Chicago, IL: University of Chicago Press.

Harter, J. & Pendell, R. (2025). "Global Engagement Falls for the Second Time Since 2009." Gallup, April 22, 2025. https://www.gallup.com/workplace/659279/global-engagement-falls-second-time-2009.aspx.

Hastings, H. (2022, June 7). Customer value is all that matters in business. *Hunter Hastings*. https://hunterhastings.com/customer-value-is-all-that-matters-in-business/.

Hamel, G. A. (2020). *Humanocracy*. Boston: HBS.

Handu's Journey to Success. (2024). *Who Knows China*, October, whoknowschina.com/case-study/handu-journey-to-success/.

Hastings, H. (2024a). *Digital Enablement: Customer-led Business, Subjective Value and Empathy*, September 20. https://hunterhastings.substack.com.

Hastings, H. a. (2024b). *Aberrant Capitalism: The Decay and Revival of Customer Capitalism*. Cambridge: Cambridge University Press.

Hayek, F. A. (1948). *Individualism and economic order*. Chicago, IL: University of Chicago Press.

Hillix, W. A., & L'Abate, L. (2012). The role of paradigms in science and theory construction. In L. L'Abate (Ed.), *Paradigms in Theory Construction* (pp. 3–16). New York, NY: Springer. https://doi.org/10.1007/978-1-4614-0914-4_1.

Jensen, M. C. (1998). *Foundations of Organizational Strategy*. Boston, MA: Harvard University Press.

Juarrero, A. (2023). *Context Changes Everything: How Constraints Create Coherence*. Cambridge: The MIT Press.

Kanter, R. M. (2018). *Haier: Incubating Entrepreneurs in a Chinese Giant*. Boston, MA: Harvard Business School.

Kaplan, R. S. (1996). *The Balanced Scorecard*. Boston, MA: Harvard Business Review Press.

Keltner, D. (2016). *The Power Paradox: How We Gain and Lose Influence.* New York: Penguin Random House.

Kirkpatrick, D. (2018). Keynote: Managing Complexity with Simplicity. *Agile People Conference.* Stockholm: YouTube, October 25.

Kirkpatrick, D. (2024a). CEO, Dartagnan Advisors. (H. Hastings, Interviewer), August 26.

Kirkpatrick, D. (2024b). *Watch Your Language: The Hidden Power of Words in the Workplace,* September 29. www.corporate-rebels.com/blog/watch-your-language-hidden-powerwords-workplace?utm_source=social&utm_medium=linkedin&utm_campaign=cr.

Kotter, J. P. (2012). *Leading Change.* Boston, MA: HBR Press.

KPMG. (2015). *The Added Value of Buurtzorg Relative to Other Providers of Home Care.* Netherlands.

Kuhn, T. (1962). *The Structure of Scientific Revolutions.* Chicago: The University of Chicago Press.

Lawrence, N. D. (2024). *The Atomic Human: What Makes Us Unique in the Age of AI.* New York: Public Affairs.

Lindkvist, L., Bengtsson, M., & Kärreman, D. (2024). The liberated firm: An integrative approach to a new trend in organizing. *Scandinavian Journal of Management, 40*(2), Article 101330. https://doi.org/10.1016/j.scaman.2024.101330.

Madden, B. J. (2020). *Value Creation Principles: The Pragmatic Theory of the Firm Begins with Purpose and Ends with Sustainable Capitalism.* Hoboken, NJ: John Wiley & Sons.

Madden, B. J. (2024). *My Value Creation Journey.* Naples, FL: Bartley J. Madden Foundation.

Maddux, W. W., Swaab, R. I., Tanure, B., & Williams, E. (2014). *Ricardo Semler: A revolutionary model of leadership* (Case No. INS517). Fontainebleau, France: INSEAD.

McCaffrey, M. (2021). *The Invisible Hand in Virtual Worlds: The Economic Order of Video Games.* Cambridge: Cambridge University Press.

McGilchrist, I. (2019). *The Master and His Emissary.* New Haven: Yale University Press.

McGilchrist, I. (2021). *The matter with things: Our brains, our delusions, and the unmaking of the world.* London, England: Perspectiva Press.

McGregor, D. (1985). *The Human Side of Enterprise.* New York: McGraw Hill.

Merton, R. K. (1949). *Social Theory and Social Structure.* Glencoe: Free Press.

Minnaar, J. (2016). *Corporate Rebels,* November 14. Retrieved from Morning Star's Success Story: No Bosses, No Titles, No Structural Hierarchy: www.corporate-rebels.com/blog/morning-star.

Mintzberg, H. (2008). Interview. *AMCF Annual Meeting*. New York: ConsultingNewsLine.

Mises, L. v. (1944). *Bureaucracy*. Yale, CT: Yale University Press.

Mises, L. v. (1998). *Human Action*. Auburn, AL: Mises Institute.

Nascimento, L. d. (2021). Dynamic Interactions Among Knowledge Management, Strategic Foresight, and Emerging Technologies. *Journal of Knowledge Management*, 275–297, 25 (2), 278.

Oo, K. K., & Rakthin, S. (2022). Integrative review of absorptive capacity's role in fostering organizational resilience and research agenda. *Sustainability*, *14*(19), 12570. https://doi.org/10.3390/su141912570.

Packard, M. D. (2022). *Entrepreneurial Valuation: An Entrepreneur's Guide to Getting into the Mind of Customers*. Berlin: de Gruyter.

Peek, S. (2024). The Management Theory of Mary Parker Follett. *business.com*, May 7.

Pendleton-Jullian, A. M., & Seely Brown, J. (2018). *Design unbound: Designing for emergence in a white water world* (Vols. 1–2). Cambridge, MA: MIT Press.

Puranam, P. (2025). Seeking self-organization in self-governing systems: Are we looking in the wrong place? *Journal of Organization Design*, *14*(2), 145–154. https://doi.org/10.1007/s41469-024-00183-z.

Putnam, R. (1993). The prosperous community: Social capital and public life. *The American Prospect*, 4 (13), 35–42.

Roy, N. (2023). How Discord Helps Build Brand Communities. *American Marketer*, January 23.

Schrager, James E. (2019). Three Strategy Lessons From GE's Decline. Chicago Booth Review.

Simon, Herbert A. (1996). Models Of My Life. MIT Press.

Steiber, A., & Alänge, S. (2024). *The Silicon Valley Model: Management for entrepreneurship* (2nd ed.). Springer Nature Switzerland AG. https://doi.org/10.1007/978-3-031-48405-6.

Taylor, F. W. (1911). *Principles of Scientific Management*. New York: Harper and Brother.

Tushman, M. L., & O'Reilly, C. A., III. (2013). Organizational ambidexterity: Past, present, and future. *Academy of Management Perspectives*, *27*(4), 324–338. https://doi.org/10.5465/amp.2013.0025.

Turner, J. R. (2020). *The Flow System*. Denton, TX: UNT Libraries.

Uzuegbu, C. N. (2015). Henri Fayol's 14 Principles of Management. *Journal of Information Theory and Practice*, 3 (2), 58–72.

West, G. (2017). *Scale: The Universal Laws of Growth, Innovation, Sustainability, and the Pace of Life in Organisms, Cities, Economies, and Companies.* New York: Penguin Press.

Witman, Paul D. What Gets Measured, Gets Managed: The Wells Fargo Account Opening Scandal. *Journal of Information Systems Education* 29, no. 3 (2018): 131–38. https://aisel.aisnet.org/jise/vol29/iss3/2.

Wong, M. L., Cleland, C. E., Arend, D., Jr., Bartlett, S., Cleaves, H. J., II, Demarest, H., Prabhu, A., Lunine, J. I., & Hazen, R. M. (2023). On the roles of function and selection in evolving systems. *Proceedings of the National Academy of Sciences, 120*(43), Article e2310223120. https://doi.org/10.1073/pnas.2310223120.

Wren, D. A., Bedeian, A. G., & Breeze, J. D. (2002). The foundations of Henri Fayol's administrative theory. *Management Decision, 40*(9), 906–918. https://doi.org/10.1108/00251740210441108.

Yong, A. (2025, January 26). Interview with DeepSeek founder: We're done following. It's time to lead. *The China Academy.* https://thechinaacademy.org/interview-with-deepseek-founder-were-done-following-its-time-to-lead/.

Cambridge Elements

Reinventing Capitalism

Arie Y. Lewin
Duke University

Arie Y. Lewin is Professor Emeritus of Strategy and International Business at Duke University, Fuqua School of Business. He is an Elected Fellow of the Academy of International Business and a Recipient of the Academy of Management inaugural Joanne Martin Trailblazer Award. Previously, he was Editor-in-Chief of *Management and Organization Review* (2015–2021) and the *Journal of International Business Studies* (2000–2007), founding Editor-in-Chief of Organization Science (1989–2007), and Convener of Organization Science Winter Conference (1990–2012). His research centers on studies of organizations' adaptation as co-evolutionary systems, the emergence of new organizational forms, and adaptive capabilities of innovating and imitating organizations. His current research focuses on de-globalization and decoupling, the Fourth Industrial Revolution, and the renewal of capitalism.

Till Talaulicar
University of Erfurt

Till Talaulicar holds the Chair of Organization and Management at the University of Erfurt where he is also the Dean of the Faculty of Economics, Law and Social Sciences. His main research expertise is in the areas of corporate governance and the responsibilities of the corporate sector in modern societies. Professor Talaulicar is Editor-in-Chief of *Corporate Governance: An International Review*, Senior Editor of Management and Organization Review and serves on the Editorial Board of Organization Science. Moreover, he has been Founding Member and Chairperson of the Board of the International Corporate Governance Society (2014–2020).

Editorial Advisory Board

Paul S. Adler, *University of Southern California, USA*
Ruth V. Aguilera, *Northeastern University, USA*
Christina Ahmadjian, *Hitotsubashi University, Japan*
Helena Barnard, *University of Pretoria, South Africa*
Jay Barney, *University of Utah, USA*
Jerry Davis, *University of Michigan, USA*
Steve Denning, *Forbes*
Rebecca Henderson, *Harvard University, USA*
Thomas Hutzschenreuter, *TU München, Germany*
Tarun Khanna, *Harvard University, USA*
Peter G. Klein, *Baylor University, USA*
Costas Markides, *London Business School, UK*
Anita McGahan, *University of Toronto, Canada*
Rita McGrath, *Columbia University, USA*
Heather McGregor, *Edinburgh Business School, UK*
Alan Meyer, *University of Oregon, USA*
Katrin Muff, *LUISS University Rome, Italy*
Peter Murmann, *University of St. Gallen, Switzerland*

Tsuyoshi Numagami, *Hitotsubashi University, Japan*
Margit Osterloh, *University of Basel, Switzerland*
Andreas Georg Scherer, *University of Zurich, Switzerland*
Blair Sheppard, *PwC, USA*
Jeffrey Sonnenfeld, *Yale University, USA*
John Sutton, *LSE, UK*
David Teece, *UC Berkeley, USA*
Anne S. Tsui, *University of Notre Dame, USA*
Alain Verbeke, *University of Calgary, Canada*
Henk Volberda, *University of Amsterdam, The Netherlands*
Mira Wilkins, *Florida International University, USA*
Sarah Williamson, *FCLTGlobal, USA*
Arjen van Witteloostuijn, *VU Amsterdam, The Netherlands*
George Yip, *Imperial College London, UK*

About the Series

This series seeks to feature explorations about the crisis of legitimacy facing capitalism today, including the increasing income and wealth gap, the decline of the middle class, threats to employment due to globalization and digitalization, undermined trust in institutions, discrimination against minorities, global poverty and pollution. Being grounded in a business and management perspective, the series incorporates contributions from multiple disciplines on the causes of the current crisis and potential solutions to renew capitalism.

Panmure House is the final and only remaining home of Adam Smith, Scottish philosopher and 'Father of modern economics.' Smith occupied the House between 1778 and 1790, during which time he completed the final editions of his master works: The Theory of Moral Sentiments and The Wealth of Nations. Other great luminaries and thinkers of the Scottish Enlightenment visited Smith regularly at the House across this period. Their mission is to provide a world-class twenty-first-century centre for social and economic debate and research, convening in the name of Adam Smith to effect positive change and forge global, future-focussed networks.

Cambridge Elements

Reinventing Capitalism

Elements in the Series

Reinventing Capitalism in the Digital Age
Stephen Denning

From Financialisation to Innovation in UK Big Pharma: AstraZeneca and GlaxoSmithKline
Öner Tulum, Antonio Andreoni, and William Lazonick

Comparing Capitalisms for an Unknown Future: Societal Processes and Transformative Capacity
Gordon Redding

The Future of Work in Diverse Economic Systems: The Varieties of Capitalism Perspective
Daniel Friel

Transforming our Critical Systems: How Can We Achieve the Systemic Change the World Needs?
Gerardus van der Zanden and Rozanne Henzen

Aberrant Capitalism: The Decay and Revival of Customer Capitalism
Hunter Hastings and Stephen Denning

Private Equity and the Demise of the Local: The Loss of Community Economic Power and Autonomy
Maryann Feldman and Martin Kenney

The Transformation of Boeing from Technological Leadership to Financial Engineering and Decline
Charles McMillan

The Fading Light of Democratic Capitalism: How Pervasive Cronyism and Restricted Suffrage Are Destroying Democratic Capitalism as a National Ideal ... And What To Do About It
Malcolm S. Salter

State-Owned Enterprises as Institutional Actors in Contemporary Capitalism and Beyond
Olivier Butzbach, Douglas B. Fuller, Gerhard Schnyder, and Luda Svystunova

Towards More Inclusive Varieties of Capitalism
Simon Collinson

The Post-Managerial Era of Capitalism: Organizational Design as the Next Innovation Frontier
Hunter Hastings

A full series listing is available at: www.cambridge.org/RECA

Made in the USA
Monee, IL
03 May 2026